Table of Contents

Numbers: Spanish
Los Números en Español

Directions: Match the numbers 1 - 20.

uno	six
siete	thirteen
catorce	eight
cuatro	eighteen
doce	one
dieciseis	fifteen
dos	seven
ocho	fourteen
dieciocho	two
seis	nineteen
diez	ten
diecisiete	seventeen
tres	three
quince	twenty
once	nine
cinco	twelve
trece	four
diecinueve	sixteen
nueve	eleven
veinte	five

Addition: Spanish
Add in Spanish!

"Addition" means "putting together" or adding two or more numbers to find the sum. For example, 3+5=8.

"Más" means "plus" in Spanish.

Directions: Add to find the answers.

Example: uno   más   tres = ____
                 | +   3

siete más catorce = ____   nueve más veinte = ____

cuatro más doce = ____   once más quince = ____

dieciseis más dos = ____   ocho más uno = ____

cinco más tres = ____   diez más seis = ____

tres más diez = ____

Addition

Directions: Add.
Example:

Add the ones.

```
 26
+21
  7
```

Add the tens.

```
 26
+21
 47
```

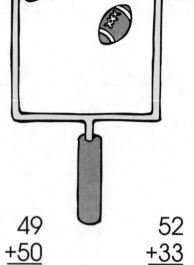

```
 18        24        38        49        52
+11       +35       +21       +50       +33
```

```
 75        83        67        44        28
+12       +16       +32       +25       +41
```

68 + 20 = _____   54 + 25 = _____   71 + 17 = _____

The Lions scored 42 points. The Clippers scored 21 points.
How many points were scored in all?   _____

Name: _____

Addition:
Football Math

Directions: Follow the plays of your favorite team.

A touchdown is worth 6 points.
A field goal is worth 3 points.

GO _____
WRITE YOUR TEAM HERE!

 2 touchdowns = _____ points

 1 touchdown + 2 field goals = _____ points

 3 field goals = _____ points

 1 field goal + 1 touchdown = _____ points

Your team won the game and made record-breaking points!
How many points did they score in all? _____

Name: _____

Subtraction

Subtraction means "taking away" or subtracting one number from another to find the difference. For example, 10 - 3 = 7.

Directions: Subtract.

Example:

Subtract the ones.

```
  39
 -24
   5
```

Subtract the tens.

```
  39
 -24
 | 5
```

```
  48        95        87        55
 -35       -22       -16       -43
```

```
  37        69        44        99
 -14       -57       -23       -78
```

66 - 44 = ____   57 - 33 = ____

The yellow car traveled 87 miles per hour. The orange car traveled 66 miles per hour. How much faster was the yellow car traveling?

_____

Place Value

The place value of a digit, or numeral, is shown by where it is in the number. For example, in the number 1,234, 1 has the place value of thousands, 2 is hundreds, 3 is tens and 4 is ones.

Hundred Thousands	Ten Thousands	Thousands	Hundreds	Tens	Ones
9	4	3	8	5	2

943,852

Directions: Match the numbers in Column A with the words in Column B.

A	B
62,453	two hundred thousand
7,641	three thousand
486,113	four hundred thousand
11,277	eight hundreds
813,463	seven tens
594,483	five ones
254,089	six hundreds
79,841	nine ten thousands
27,115	five tens

Name: _____

Place Value

Directions: Use the code to color the rings.

If the number has:

7 ten thousands, color it red.

1 thousand, color it blue.

4 hundred thousands, color it green.

6 tens, color it brown.

8 ones, color it yellow.

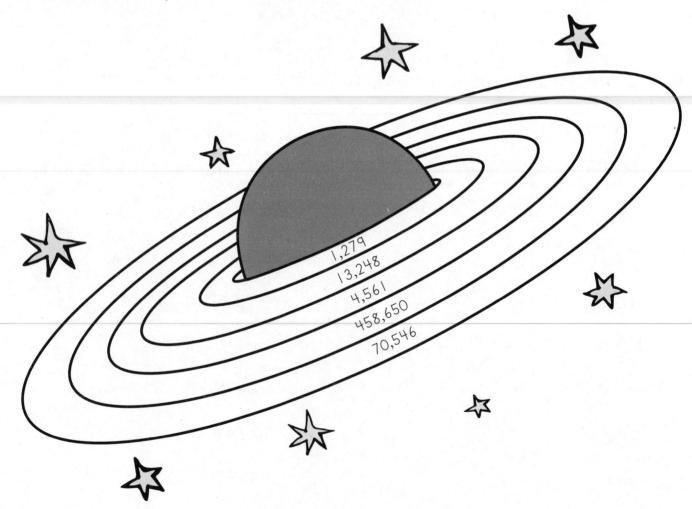

1,279
13,248
4,561
458,650
70,546

Addition: Regrouping

Addition means "putting together" or adding two or more numbers to find the sum. For example, 3 + 5 = 8. To regroup is to use ten ones to form one ten, ten tens to form one 100 and so on.

Directions: Add using regrouping.

Example:

Add the ones.	Add the tens with regrouping.
88 +21 9	88 +21 10 9

37 +72	56 +67	51 +88	37 +55	70 +68

93 +54	47 +82	81 +77	23 +92	36 +71

92 + 13 = ____   73 + 83 = ____   54 + 61 = ____

The Blues scored 63 points. The Reds scored 44 points.
How many points were scored in all?   _____

Subtraction: Regrouping

Subtraction means "taking away" or subtracting one number from another to find the difference. For example, 10 - 3 = 7. To regroup is to use one ten to form ten ones, one 100 to form ten tens and so on.

Directions: Study the example. Subtract using regrouping.

Example:

$$32 = 2\text{ tens} + 12\text{ ones}$$
$$-13 = 1\text{ ten} + 3\text{ ones}$$
$$19 = 1\text{ ten} + 9\text{ ones}$$

33 -28	86 -59	92 -37	71 -48

63 -47	45 -18	31 -22	55 -39

82 - 69 = _____   73 - 36 = _____

The Yankees won 85 games.
The Cubs won 69 games.
How many more games
did the Yankees win? _____

Name: _____

Addition And Subtraction: Regrouping

Addition means "putting together" or adding two or more numbers to find the sum. Subtraction means "taking away" or subtracting one number from another to find the difference. To regroup is to use one ten to form ten ones, one 100 to form ten tens and so on.

Directions: Add or subtract. Regroup when needed.

```
  92        58        63        77
 -47       +26       +18       -38
```

```
  27        31        56        67
 -17       +42       -29       +33
```

```
  72        87        93        54
 +19       -58       -89       +27
```

The soccer team scored 83 goals this year. The soccer team scored 68 goals last year. How many goals did they score in all? _____

How many more goals did they score this year than last year? _____

Review

Directions: Write this number on the blank:
4 hundred thousands
5 ten thousands
1 thousand
8 hundreds
3 tens
3 ones

___ ___ ___ , ___ ___ ___

Directions: Add or subtract. Use regrouping when needed.

$$\begin{array}{r} 87 \\ -18 \\ \hline \end{array} \qquad \begin{array}{r} 45 \\ +29 \\ \hline \end{array} \qquad \begin{array}{r} 95 \\ -27 \\ \hline \end{array} \qquad \begin{array}{r} 32 \\ +19 \\ \hline \end{array}$$

$$\begin{array}{r} 86 \\ -59 \\ \hline \end{array} \qquad \begin{array}{r} 66 \\ -39 \\ \hline \end{array} \qquad \begin{array}{r} 74 \\ +23 \\ \hline \end{array} \qquad \begin{array}{r} 92 \\ -67 \\ \hline \end{array}$$

57 + 18 = ____   42 - 33 = ____   35 + 19 = ____

Sue won 75 tennis games. Jim won 59 tennis games.
How many more games did Sue win?   _____

Addition: Regrouping

Directions: Study the example. Add using regrouping.

Examples:

Add the ones. Regroup.

```
  1
 156        6
+267       +7
  3        13
```

Add the tens. Regroup.

```
  1      11
  5      156
 +6     +267
 12      23
```

Add the hundreds.

```
  1
 156
+267
 423
```

```
 29        81        52        49
 46        78        67        37        162
+12       +33       +23       +19       +349
```

```
273       655       783       385       428
+198      +297      +148      +169      +122
```

Sally went bowling. She had scores of 115, 129 and 103. What was her total score for three games? _____

Addition: Regrouping

Directions: Add using regrouping. Then use the code to discover the name of a United States president.

348 +752 1,100	642 +277	386 +787	184 +875	578 +874

653 +768	653 +359	946 +239	393 +257	199 +843

721
+679

____ . ___ ___ ___ ___ ___ ___ ___ ___ ___

1012	1173	1059	1421	919	650	1452	1042	1100	1400	1185
N	A	S	I	W	T	H	O	G	N	G

Name: _____

Addition: Regrouping

Directions: Study the example. Add using regrouping.

Example:

Steps:

5,356
+3,976
9,332

1. Add the ones.
2. Regroup the tens. Add the tens.
3. Regroup the hundreds. Add the hundreds.
4. Add the thousands.

6,849   1,846   9,221
+3,276   +8,384   +6,769

2,758   5,299   7,932
+3,663   +8,764   +6,879

A plane flew 1,838 miles on the first day. It flew 2,347 miles on the second day. How many miles did it fly in all?

_____

Addition: Mental Math

Directions: Try to do these addition problems in your head without using paper and pencil.

7	6	8	10	2	6
+4	+3	+1	+ 2	+9	+6

10	40	80	60	50	100
+20	+20	+100	+30	+70	+ 40

350	300	400	450	680	900
+150	+500	+800	+ 10	+100	+ 70

	4,000	300	8,000		7,000
1,000	400	200	500	9,800	300
+ 200	+ 30	+ 80	+ 60	+ 150	+ 30

Subtraction: Regrouping

Directions: Regrouping for subtraction is the opposite of regrouping for addition. Study the example. Subtract using regrouping. Then use the code to color the flowers.

Example:

```
 647
-453
 194
```

Steps:
1. Subtract ones.
2. Subtract tens. Five tens cannot be subtracted from 4 tens.
3. Regroup tens by regrouping 6 hundreds
   (5 hundreds + 10 tens).
4. Add the 10 tens to the four tens.
5. Subtract 5 tens from 14 tens.
6. Subtract the hundreds.

If the answer has:
1 one, color it red;
8 ones, color it pink;
5 ones, color it yellow.

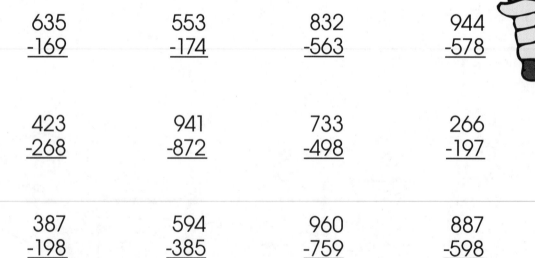

Subtraction: Regrouping

Directions: Study the example. Follow the steps. Subtract using regrouping.

Example:

634
-455
179

Steps:
1. Subtract ones. You cannot subtract five ones from 4 ones.
2. Regroup ones by regrouping 3 tens to 2 tens + 10 ones.
3. Subtract 5 ones from 14 ones.
4. Regroup tens by regrouping hundreds (5 hundreds + 10 tens).
5. Subtract 5 tens from 12 tens.
6. Subtract hundreds.

635	553	832	944
-169	-174	-563	-578

423	941	733	266
-268	-872	-498	-197

387	594	960	887
-198	-385	-759	-598

Sue goes to school 185 days a year. Yoko goes to school 313 days a year. How many more days of school does Yoko attend each year?

_____

Subtraction: Regrouping

Directions: Study the example. Follow the steps. Subtract using regrouping. If you have to regroup to subtract ones and there are no tens, you must regroup twice.

Example:

```
 300
-182
 118
```

Steps:
1. Subtract ones. You cannot subtract 2 ones from 0 ones.
2. Regroup. No tens. Regroup hundreds
   (2 hundreds + 10 tens).
3. Regroup tens (9 tens + 10 ones).
4. Subtract 2 ones from ten ones.
5. Subtract 8 tens from 9 tens.
6. Subtract 1 hundred from 2 hundreds.

602	306	600	807	703
-423	-128	-263	-499	-328

800	206	400	508	909
-557	-137	-224	-379	-769

207	604	308	700	900
-138	-397	-199	-531	-278

Subtraction: Regrouping

Directions: Subtract. Regroup when necessary. The first one is done for you.

7,354	4,214	8,437	6,837
-5,295	-3,185	-5,338	-4,318
2,059			

5,735	1,036	6,735	3,841
-3,826	- 947	-6,646	-1,953

Columbus discovered America in 1492. The pilgrims landed in America in 1620. How many years difference was there between these two events?

_____

Subtraction: Mental Math

Directions: Try to do these subtraction problems in your head without using paper and pencil.

9 - 3	12 - 6	7 - 6	5 - 1	15 - 5	2 - 0

40 - 20	90 - 80	100 - 50	20 - 20	60 - 10	70 - 40

450 - 250	500 - 300	250 - 20	690 - 100	320 - 20	900 - 600

1,000 - 400	8,000 - 500	7,000 - 900	4,000 - 2,000	9,500 - 4,000	5,000 - 2,000

Name: _____

Review

Directions: Add or subtract using regrouping.

28	82	33	67
56	49	75	94
+93	+51	+128	+248

683	756	818	956
-495	+139	-387	+267

1,588	4,675	8,732	2,938
- 989	-2,976	-5,664	+3,459

To drive from New York City to Los Angeles is 2,832 miles. To drive from New York City to Miami is 1,327 miles. How much farther is it to drive from New York City to Los Angeles than from New York City to Miami? _____

Rounding: The Nearest Ten

If the ones number is 5 or greater, "round up" to the nearest 10. If the ones number is 4 or less, the tens number stays the same and the ones number becomes a zero.

Examples: 15 round up to 20   23 round down to 20   47 round up to 50

7 _____

12 _____

33 _____

27 _____

73 _____

25 _____

39 _____

58 _____

81 _____

94 _____

44 _____

88 _____

66 _____

70 _____

Rounding: The Nearest Hundred

If the tens number is 5 or greater, "round up" to the nearest hundred.
If the tens number is 4 or less, the hundreds number remains the same.

REMEMBER... Look at the number directly to the right of the place you are rounding to.

Example:

2<u>3</u>0 round <u>down</u> to 200   4<u>7</u>0 round <u>up</u> to 500

1<u>5</u>0 round <u>up</u> to 200   7<u>3</u>2 round <u>down</u> to 700

456 ____	120 ____
340 ____	923 ____
867 ____	550 ____
686 ____	231 ____
770 ____	492 ____

Front-End Estimation

Front-end estimation is useful when you don't need to know the exact amount, but a close answer will do.

When we use front-end estimation, we use only the first number, and then add the numbers together to get the estimate.

Example:

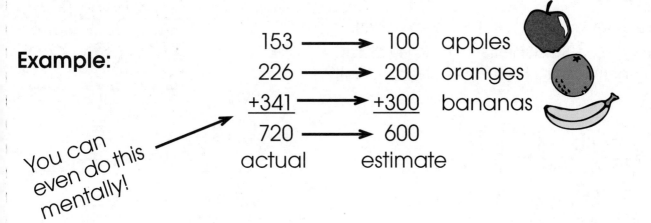

You can even do this mentally!

153	→	100	apples
226	→	200	oranges
+341	→	+300	bananas
720	→	600	
actual		estimate	

Directions: Estimate the sum of these numbers.

```
 456 ⟶              910 ⟶              686 ⟶
 121 ⟶              280 ⟶              307 ⟶
+438 ⟶    +____    +320 ⟶    +____    +711 ⟶    +____

          ┌────┐            ┌────┐            ┌────┐
          │    │            │    │            │    │
          └────┘            └────┘            └────┘
```

Multiplication

Multiplication is a short way to find the sum of adding the same number a certain amount of times. For example, we write 7 x 4 = 28 instead of 7 + 7 + 7 + 7 = 28.

Directions: Study the example. Multiply.

Example:

There are two groups of seashells.
There are 3 seashells in each group.   2 x 3 = 6
How many seashells are there in all?

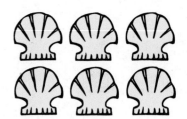

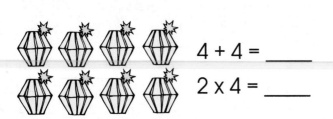

4 + 4 = _____

2 x 4 = _____

3 + 3 + 3 = _____

3 x 3 = _____

$$
\begin{array}{ccccc}
2 & 3 & 4 & 6 & 7 \\
\underline{\times 3} & \underline{\times 5} & \underline{\times 3} & \underline{\times 2} & \underline{\times 3}
\end{array}
$$

$$
\begin{array}{ccccc}
5 & 6 & 4 & 7 & 8 \\
\underline{\times 2} & \underline{\times 3} & \underline{\times 2} & \underline{\times 2} & \underline{\times 3}
\end{array}
$$

$$
\begin{array}{ccccc}
5 & 9 & 8 & 6 & 9 \\
\underline{\times 5} & \underline{\times 4} & \underline{\times 5} & \underline{\times 6} & \underline{\times 3}
\end{array}
$$

Multiplication

Directions: Multiply.

$$
\begin{array}{c} 3 \\ \underline{\times 5} \end{array}
\qquad
\begin{array}{c} 4 \\ \underline{\times 6} \end{array}
\qquad
\begin{array}{c} 3 \\ \underline{\times 8} \end{array}
$$

$$
\begin{array}{c} 5 \\ \underline{\times 5} \end{array}
\qquad
\begin{array}{c} 4 \\ \underline{\times 8} \end{array}
\qquad
\begin{array}{c} 5 \\ \underline{\times 4} \end{array}
$$

$$
\begin{array}{c} 6 \\ \underline{\times 7} \end{array}
\quad
\begin{array}{c} 3 \\ \underline{\times 9} \end{array}
\quad
\begin{array}{c} 2 \\ \underline{\times 8} \end{array}
\quad
\begin{array}{c} 7 \\ \underline{\times 6} \end{array}
\quad
\begin{array}{c} 9 \\ \underline{\times 4} \end{array}
$$

$$
\begin{array}{c} 6 \\ \underline{\times 8} \end{array}
\quad
\begin{array}{c} 5 \\ \underline{\times 6} \end{array}
\quad
\begin{array}{c} 7 \\ \underline{\times 7} \end{array}
\quad
\begin{array}{c} 5 \\ \underline{\times 3} \end{array}
\quad
\begin{array}{c} 8 \\ \underline{\times 9} \end{array}
$$

A river boat makes 3 trips a day every day.
How many trips does it make in a week?

_____

Name: _____

Multiplication

Factors are the numbers multiplied together in a multiplication problem. The answer is called the product. If you change the order of the factors, the product stays the same.

Example:

There are 4 groups of fish.
There are 3 fish in each group.
How many fish are there in all?

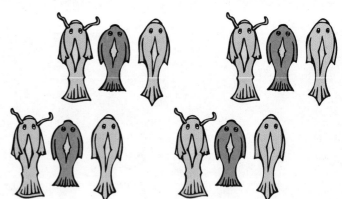

$$4 \times 3 = 12$$
factor x factor = product

Directions: Draw 3 groups of 4 fish.

$$3 \times 4 = 12$$

Compare your drawing and answer with the example. What did you notice?

Directions: Fill in the missing numbers. Multiply.

5 x 4 = _____   3 x 6 = _____   4 x 2= _____

4 x 5 = _____   6 x 3 = _____   2 x 4 = _____

| 3
x7 | 7
x3 | 2
x9 | 9
x2 | 8
x4 | 4
x8 |

| 5
x2 | 2
x5 | 6
x3 | 3
x6 | 5
x6 | 6
x5 |

Multiplication: Zero And One

Any number multiplied by zero equals zero. One multiplied by any number equals that number. Study the example. Multiply.

Example:

How many full sails are there in all?

2 boats x **1** sail on each boat = **2** sails

How many full sails are there now?

2 boats x **0** sails = **0** sails

Directions: Multiply.

1	2	3	4	0	7
x5	x1	x0	x1	x6	x0

9	8	3	4	7	6
x1	x0	x1	x0	x1	x1

Multiplication

Directions: Time yourself as you multiply. How quickly can you complete this page?

3 x2	8 x7	1 x0	1 x6	3 x4	0 x4

4 x1	4 x4	2 x5	9 x3	9 x9	5 x3

0 x8	2 x6	9 x6	8 x5	7 x3	4 x2

3 x5	2 x0	4 x6	1 x3	0 x0	3 x3

Name: _____

Multiplication Table

Directions: Complete the multiplication table. Use it to practice your multiplication facts.

X	0	1	2	3	4	5	6	7	8	9	10
0	0										
1		1									
2			4								
3				9							
4					16						
5						25					
6							36				
7								49			
8									64		
9										81	
10											100

Division

Division is a way to find out how many times one number is contained in another number. For example, 28 ÷ 4 = 7 means that there are seven groups of four in 28.

Directions: Study the example. Divide.

Example:

There are 6 oars.
Each canoe needs 2 oars.
How many canoes can be used?

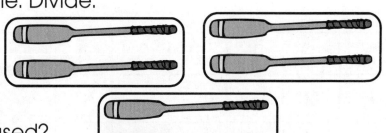

Circle groups of 2.
There are 3 groups of 2.

6 ÷ 2 = 3
oars   number   canoes
       of oars
       needed
       per canoe

9 ÷ 3 = ____   8 ÷ 2 = ____   16 ÷ 4 = ____

15 ÷ 5 = ____   18 ÷ 2 = ____   20 ÷ 4 = ____

21 ÷ 7 = ____   24 ÷ 6 = ____   12 ÷ 2= ____

Name:_____

Division

Directions: Divide. Draw a line from the boat to the sail with the correct answer.

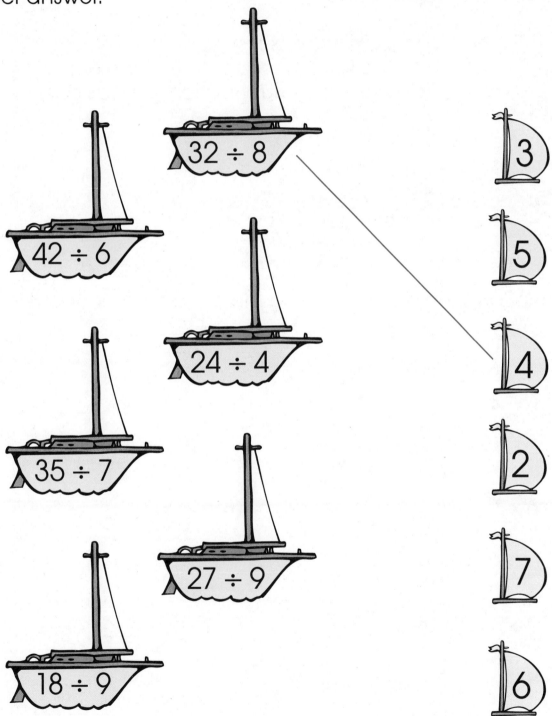

Order of Operations

When you solve a problem that involves more than one operation, this is the order to follow:

()   Parentheses first
x   Multiplication and ÷ Division (left to right)
+   Addition – Subtraction (left to right)

Example:

$$2 + (3 \times 5) - 2 = 15$$
$$2 + 15 - 2 = 15$$
$$17 - 2 = 15$$

Directions: Solve the problems using the correct order of operations.

$(5 - 3) + 4 \times 7 =$ _____ $1 + 2 \times 3 + 4 =$ _____

$6 \times 3 - 1 =$ _____ $(8 \div 2) \times 4 =$ _____

$9 \div 3 \times 3 + 0 =$ _____ $5 - 2 + 2 =$ _____

Order of Operations

Directions: Use +, –, x and ÷ to complete the problems so the number sentence is true.

Example: 4 __+__ 2 __–__ 1 = 5

(8 ____ 2) ____ 4 = 8

(1 ____ 2) ____ 3 = 1

9 ____ 3 ____ 9 = 3

(7 ____ 5) ____ 1 = 2

8 ____ 5 ____ 4 = 10

5 ____ 4 ____ 1 = .1

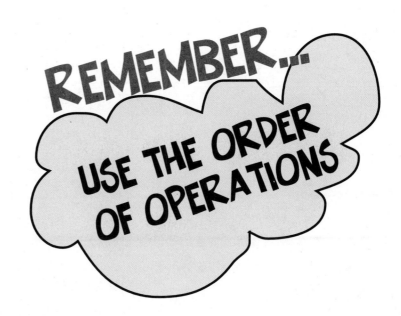

REMEMBER...
USE THE ORDER OF OPERATIONS

Name: _____

Review

Directions: Multiply or divide. Fill in the blanks with the missing numbers or x or ÷ signs. The first one is done for you.

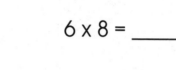

5 <u>x</u> 4 = 20

6 x 8 = ____

7 x ____ = 14

3 _ 6 = 18

7 x 2 = ____

____ x 3 = 24

6 _ 2 = 3

24 ÷ 6 = ____

6 x 5 = ____

25 _ 5 = 5

49 ÷ 7 = ____

8 x ____ = 32

3 _ 8 = 24

18 ÷ 3 = ____

9 x 5 = ____

12 _ 3 = 4

9 x 8 = ____

6 x ____ = 36

Division

Division is a way to find out how many times one number is contained in another number. The ÷ sign means "divided by." Another way to divide is to use ⌐‾. The dividend is the larger number that is divided by the smaller number, or divisor. The answer of a division problem is called the quotient.

Directions: Study the example. Divide.

Example:

$$20 \div 4 = 5$$

dividend   divisor   quotient

quotient
↕
$$4 \overline{)20}$$
↕   ↕
divisor   dividend

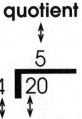

$$35 \div 7 = \underline{}$$ $$7 \overline{)35}$$ $$42 \div 6 = \underline{}$$ $$6 \overline{)42}$$

$$2 \overline{)12}$$ $$3 \overline{)18}$$ $$4 \overline{)36}$$ $$5 \overline{)50}$$

$$6 \overline{)24}$$ $$7 \overline{)21}$$ $$8 \overline{)32}$$ $$9 \overline{)27}$$

$$36 \div 6 = \underline{}$$ $$28 \div 4 = \underline{}$$ $$15 \div 5 = \underline{}$$ $$12 \div 2 = \underline{}$$

A tree farm has 36 trees. There are 4 rows of trees. How many trees are there in each row? _____

Division: Zero And One

Directions: Study the rules of division and the examples. Divide, then write the number of the rule you used to solve each problem.

Examples:

Rule 1: $1\overline{)5}$ (quotient 5)   Any number divided by 1 is that number.

Rule 2: $5\overline{)5}$ (quotient 1)   Any number except 0 divided by itself is 1.

Rule 3: $7\overline{)0}$ (quotient 0)   Zero divided by any number is zero.

Rule 4: $0\overline{)7}$ You cannot divide by zero.

$1\overline{)6}$ Rule ____ $4 \div 1 =$ ____   Rule ____

$7\overline{)7}$ Rule ____ $9 \div 9 =$ ____   Rule ____

ZERO ONE

$9\overline{)0}$ Rule ____ $7 \div 1 =$ ____   Rule ____

$1\overline{)4}$ Rule ____ $6 \div 0 =$ ____   Rule ____

Division: Remainders

Division is a way to find out how many times one number is contained in another number. For example, 28 ÷ 4 = 7 means that there are seven groups of four in 28. The dividend is the larger number that is divided by the smaller number, or divisor. The quotient is the answer in a division problem. The remainder is the amount left over. The remainder is always less than the divisor.

Directions: Study the example. Find each quotient and remainder.

Example:

There are 11 dog biscuits. Put them in groups of 3. There are 2 left over.

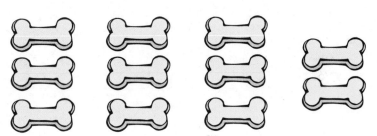

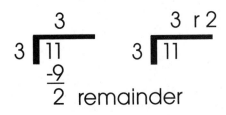

Remember: The remainder must be less than the **divisor**!

$$3 \overline{)13} \qquad 4 \overline{)17} \qquad 6 \overline{)32} \qquad 5 \overline{)26}$$

9 ÷ 4 = _____   12 ÷ 5 = _____   26 ÷ 4 = _____   49 ÷ 9 = _____

The pet store has 7 cats. Two cats go in each cage. How many cats are left over?

_____

Multiples

Directions: Draw a red circle around the numbers that can be divided by 2. We say these are multiples of 2.
Draw a blue **X** on the multiples of 3.
Draw a green square around the multiples of 5.
Draw a yellow circle around the multiples of 10.

1	2	3	4	5	6	7	8	9	10
11	12	13	14	15	16	17	18	19	20
21	22	23	24	25	26	27	28	29	30
31	32	33	34	35	36	37	38	39	40
41	42	43	44	45	46	47	48	49	50
51	52	53	54	55	56	57	58	59	60
61	62	63	64	65	66	67	68	69	70
71	72	73	74	75	76	77	78	79	80
81	82	83	84	85	86	87	88	89	90
91	92	93	94	95	96	97	98	99	100

Look at your chart. Common multiples are those which are shared. You have marked them in more than one way/color. What numbers are common?_____

Divisibility Rules

A number is divisible... by 2 if the last digit is 0 or even (2, 4, 6, 8).
by 3 if the sum of all digits is divisible by 3.
by 4 if the last two digits are divisible by 4.
by 5 if the last digit is a 0 or 5.
by 10 if the last digit is 0.

Example: 250 is divisible by <u>2, 5, 10</u>

Directions: Tell what numbers each of these numbers is divisible by.

3,732 _____   439 _____

50 _____   444 _____

7,960 _____   8,212 _____

104,924 _____   2,345 _____

Name:_____

Factor Trees

Factors are the smaller numbers multiplied together to make a larger number. Factor trees are one way to find all the factors of a number.

Example:

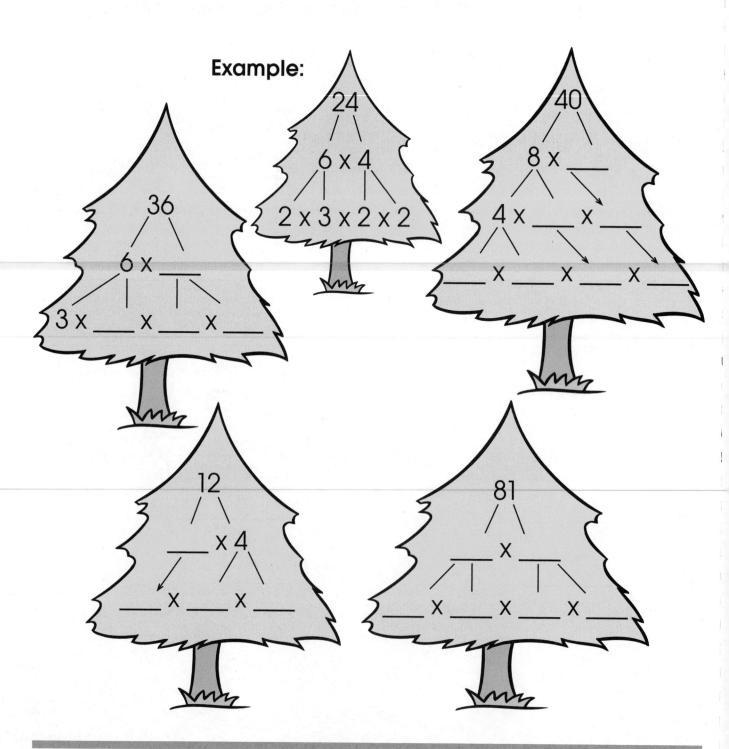

24
6 x 4
2 x 3 x 2 x 2

40
8 x ___
4 x ___ x ___
___ x ___ x ___ x ___

36
6 x ___
3 x ___ x ___ x ___

12
___ x 4
___ x ___ x ___ x ___

81
___ x ___
___ x ___ x ___ x ___

Percentages

A percentage is the amount of a number out of 100. This is the percent sign: %

Directions: Fill in the blanks.

Example: $70\% = \dfrac{70}{100}$

$\underline{40}\% = \dfrac{40}{100}$

$30\% = \dfrac{}{100}$

$10\% = \dfrac{}{100}$

$90\% = \dfrac{}{100}$

$40\% = \dfrac{}{100}$

$70\% = \dfrac{}{100}$

$80\% = \dfrac{}{100}$

$\underline{}\% = \dfrac{20}{100}$

$\underline{}\% = \dfrac{60}{100}$

$\underline{}\% = \dfrac{30}{100}$

$\underline{}\% = \dfrac{10}{100}$

$\underline{}\% = \dfrac{50}{100}$

$\underline{}\% = \dfrac{90}{100}$

Name: _____

Fractions

A fraction is a number that names part of a whole, such as $\frac{1}{2}$ or $\frac{1}{3}$.

Directions: Write the fraction that tells what part of each figure is colored. The first one is done for you.

Example:

      2 parts shaded
      5 parts in the whole figure

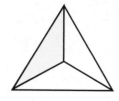

$\frac{1}{3}$

_____

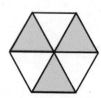

_____

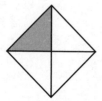

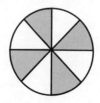

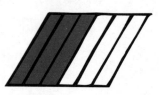

_____

Name:_____

Fractions

Directions: We often use fractions in cooking or baking. Look for fractions you know as you use this recipe with your mom or dad.

CHOCOLATE CHIP COOKIES

Cream: 1 cup shortening   1 cup brown sugar
$\frac{1}{2}$ cup sugar   1 teaspoon vanilla

Add: 2 eggs, one at a time. Beat
well after each egg is added.

Sift: $2\frac{1}{4}$ cups flour   1 teaspoon salt
1 teaspoon baking soda

Add sifted ingredients to creamed mixture.

Stir: in 2 cups of chocolate chips

Bake: at 350 degrees in an oven for 10 minutes on
ungreased cookie sheets

Challenge: Double the recipe and see what happens to
the fractions!

Fractions: Equivalent

Fractions that name the same part of a whole are equivalent fractions.

Example:

$$\frac{1}{2} = \frac{2}{4}$$

Directions: Fill in the numbers to complete the equivalent fractions.

$$\frac{1}{4} = \frac{\boxed{}}{8}$$

$$\frac{2}{3} = \frac{\boxed{}}{6}$$

$$\frac{1}{6} = \frac{\boxed{}}{12}$$

$$\frac{2}{3} = \frac{\boxed{}}{6}$$

$$\frac{1}{3} = \frac{\boxed{}}{12}$$

$$\frac{1}{5} = \frac{\boxed{}}{15}$$

$$\frac{1}{4} = \frac{\boxed{}}{8}$$

$$\frac{1}{2} = \frac{\boxed{}}{6}$$

$$\frac{2}{3} = \frac{\boxed{}}{9}$$

$$\frac{2}{6} = \frac{\boxed{}}{18}$$

Name: _____

Fractions: Division

A fraction is a number that names part of an object. It can also name part of a group.

Directions: Study the example. Divide by the bottom number of the fraction to find the answers.

Example:
There are 6 cheerleaders.
$\frac{1}{2}$ of the cheerleaders are boys.
How many cheerleaders are boys?

6 cheerleaders ÷ 2 groups = 3 boys

$\frac{1}{2}$ of 6 = 3

$\frac{1}{2}$ of 8 = ___4___

$\frac{1}{2}$ of 10 = ____

$\frac{1}{3}$ of 9 = ____

$\frac{1}{5}$ of 10 = ____

$\frac{1}{4}$ of 12 = ____

$\frac{1}{8}$ of 32 = ____

$\frac{1}{3}$ of 27 = ____

$\frac{1}{5}$ of 30 = ____

$\frac{1}{2}$ of 14 = ____

$\frac{1}{9}$ of 18 = ____

$\frac{1}{6}$ of 24 = ____

$\frac{1}{3}$ of 18 = ____

$\frac{1}{10}$ of 50 = ____

Fractions: Comparing

Directions: Circle the fraction in each pair that is larger.

Example:

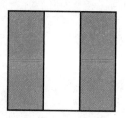

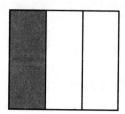

$\dfrac{2}{3}$ (circled)

$\dfrac{1}{3}$

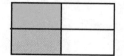

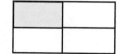

$\dfrac{2}{4}$

$\dfrac{1}{4}$

$\dfrac{1}{8}$

$\dfrac{2}{8}$

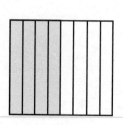

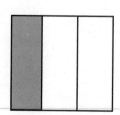

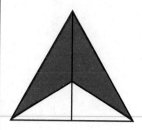

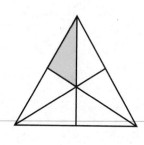

$\dfrac{1}{2}$

$\dfrac{1}{3}$

$\dfrac{2}{3}$

$\dfrac{1}{6}$

$\dfrac{1}{4}$ or $\dfrac{1}{6}$

$\dfrac{1}{5}$ or $\dfrac{1}{7}$

$\dfrac{1}{8}$ or $\dfrac{1}{4}$

Review

Directions: Divide. Draw a line from each problem to the correct answer.

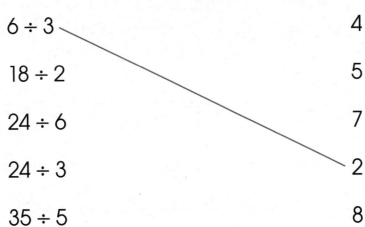

6 ÷ 3   4

18 ÷ 2   5

24 ÷ 6   7

24 ÷ 3   2

35 ÷ 5   8

45 ÷ 9   9

Directions: Divide.

$\frac{1}{3}$ of 12 = ____ $\frac{1}{4}$ of 20 = ____ $\frac{1}{5}$ of 15 = ____

$\frac{1}{6}$ of 18 = ____ $\frac{1}{7}$ of 28 = ____ $\frac{1}{9}$ of 27 = ____

Directions: Color parts of each object to match the fractions given.

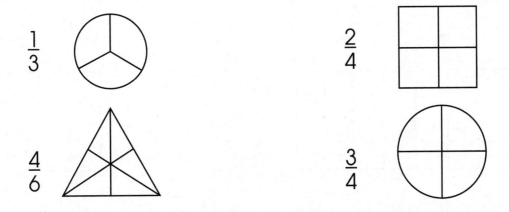

$\frac{1}{3}$

$\frac{4}{6}$

$\frac{2}{4}$

$\frac{3}{4}$

Decimals

A decimal is a number with one or more numbers to the right of a decimal point. A decimal point is a dot placed between the ones place and the tens place of a number, such as 2.5.

Example:

$\frac{3}{10}$ can be written as .3   They are both read as three-tenths.

Directions: Write the answer as a decimal for the shaded parts.

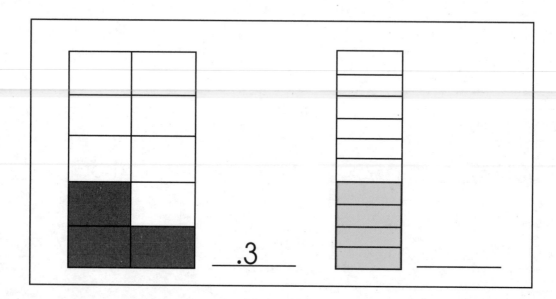

Directions: Color parts of each object to match the decimals given.

.7   .6   .5

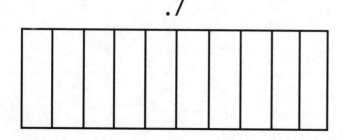
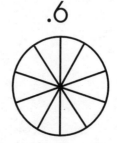
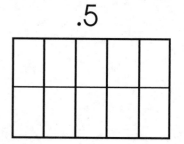

Name: _____

Decimals

A decimal is a number with one or more numbers to the right of a decimal point, such as 6.5 or 2.25. Equivalent means numbers that are equal.

Directions: Draw a line between the equivalent numbers.

.8	$\dfrac{5}{10}$
five-tenths	$\dfrac{8}{10}$
.7	$\dfrac{6}{10}$
.4	.3
six-tenths	$\dfrac{2}{10}$
three-tenths	$\dfrac{7}{10}$
.2	$\dfrac{9}{10}$
nine-tenths	$\dfrac{4}{10}$

Name: _____

Decimals Greater Than 1

Directions: Write the decimal for the part that is shaded.

Example: $2\frac{4}{10}$

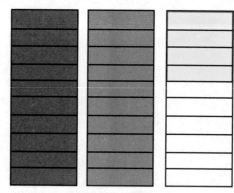

Write: 2.4   Read: two and four-tenths

$1\frac{2}{10}$ = _____

$3\frac{6}{10}$ = _____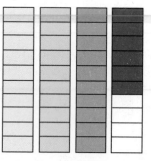

$2\frac{3}{10}$ = _____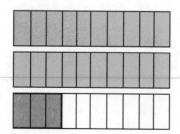

$2\frac{7}{10}$ = _____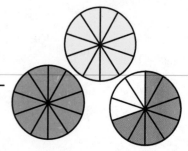

Directions: Write each number as a decimal.

four and two-tenths = _____   seven and one-tenth = _____

$3\frac{4}{10}$ = _____ $6\frac{9}{10}$ = _____ $8\frac{3}{10}$ = _____ $7\frac{5}{10}$ = _____

Decimals: Addition And Subtraction

Decimals are added and subtracted in the same way as other numbers. Simply carry down the decimal point to your answer.

Directions: Add or subtract.

Examples:

```
   1
   1.3              4.5
 + 2.8            - 2.2
 ─────            ─────
   4.1              2.3
```

```
   1.3              4.6              5.1              6.7
 + 2.2            - 3.4            + 8.8            - 4.3
 ─────            ─────            ─────            ─────
```

```
   7.9              6.4             11.4              0.5
 - 3.7            + 8.7            - 9.5            + 3.6
 ─────            ─────            ─────            ─────
```

9.3 + 1.2 = _____   2.5 - 0.7 = _____   1.2 + 5.0 = _____

Bob jogs around the school every day. The distance for one time around is .7 of a mile. If he jogs around the school two times, how many miles does he jog each day? _____

Patterns

Directions: Write the one that would come next in each pattern.

0 2 0 4 0 6   _____

1 3 5 7 9 11   _____

5 10 20 40 80   _____

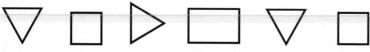 _____

 _____

○ ○ ● ● ○ ○   _____

1 A 2 B 3 C   _____

A B C 1 2 3   _____

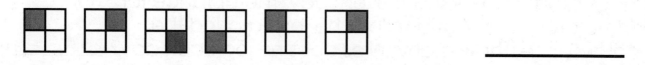 _____

Name: _____

Pattern Maze

Directions: Follow the pattern: ● ■ ▲ ☆ to get through the maze.

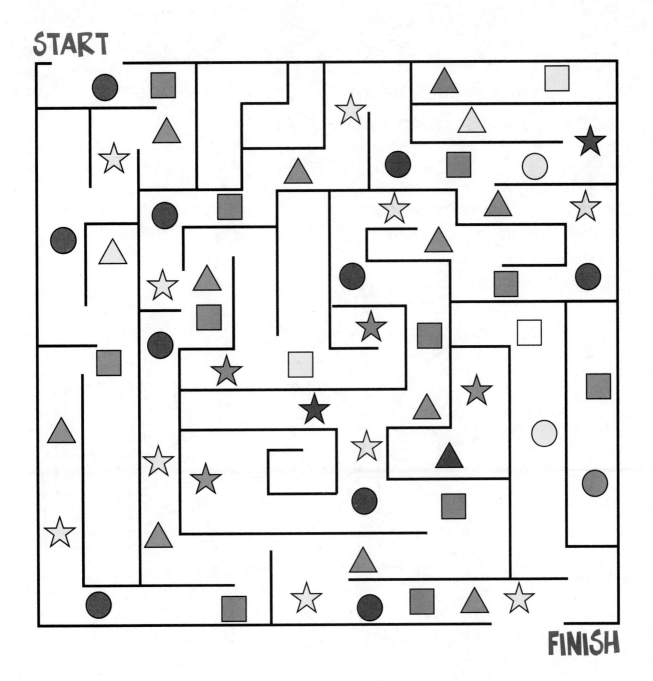

Name:_____

Geometry

Geometry is the branch of mathematics that has to do with points, lines and shapes.

  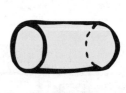 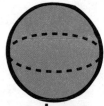

cube **rectangular prism** **cone** **cylinder** **sphere**

Directions: Use the code to color the picture.

Color:
cubes — blue
rectangular prisms — red
cones — green
cylinders — yellow
spheres —orange

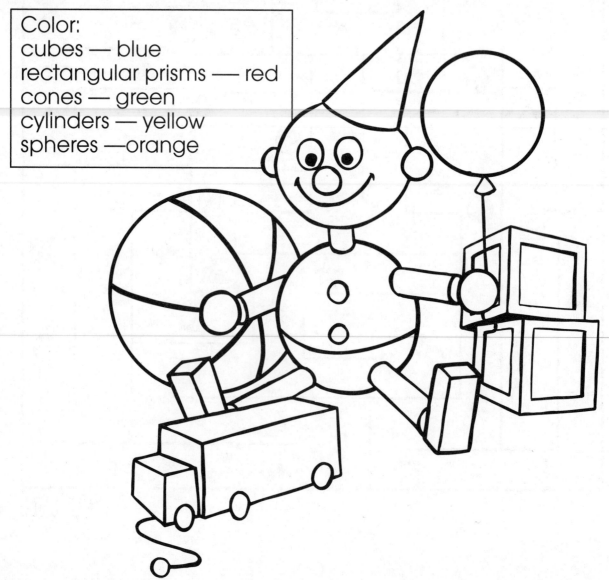

Name:_____

Geometry

Directions: Circle the patterns below that create a box when folded.

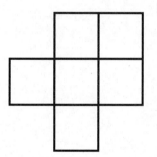

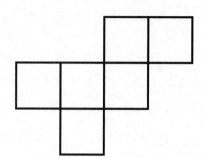

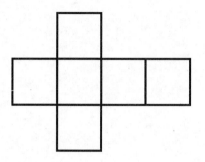

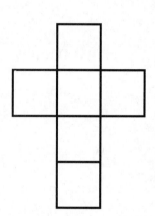

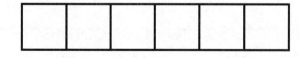

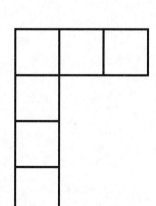

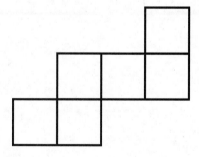

Geometry

Directions: Answer the questions.

 How many triangles do you see? ____

 How many squares in this figure? ____

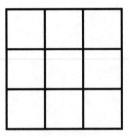

How many line segments can be drawn to connect the four dots? ____

Tangram

Directions: Cut out the tangram below. Use the shapes to make a cat, a chicken, a boat and a large triangle.

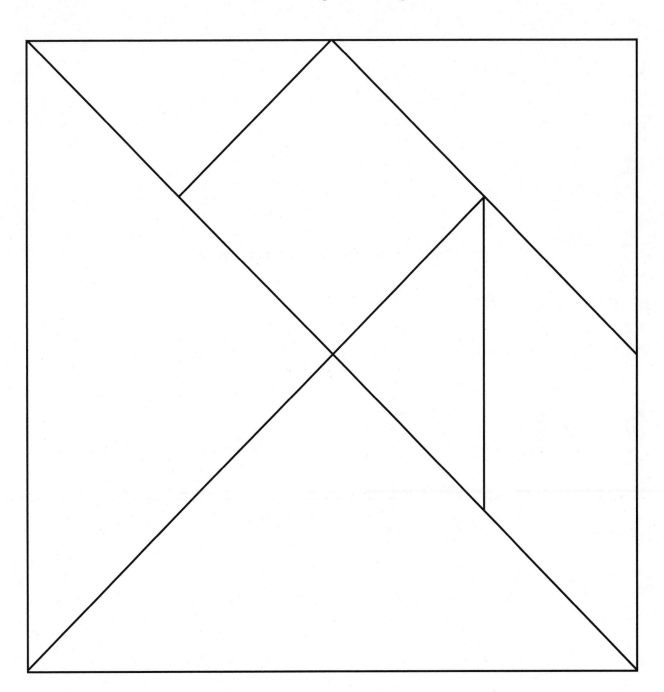

Page is blank for cutting exercise on previous page.

Name: _____

Geometry Challenge

Directions: 1. Draw 4 squares.
2. Draw as many possibilities of them touching one edge as you can.

Example:

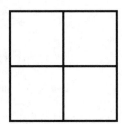 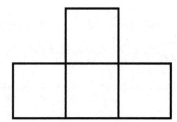

Directions: Count all the triangles.

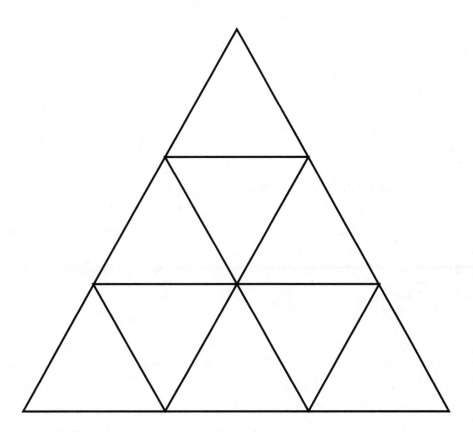

There are _____ triangles in the figure above.

Name:_____

Geometry: Lines Segments, Rays, Angles

Geometry is the branch of mathematics that has to do with points, lines and shapes.

A **line** goes on and on in both directions. It has no end points.

   Line CD

A **segment** is part of a line. It has two end points.

   Segment AB

A **ray** has a line segment with only one end point. It goes on and on in the other direction.

   Ray EF

An **angle** has two rays with the same end point.

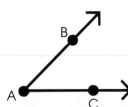   Angle BAC

Directions: Write the name for each figure.

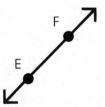   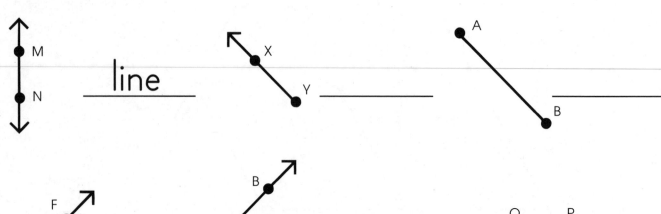

line _____

_____   _____   _____

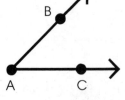

Geometry Game

Directions: 1. Cut out the cards at the bottom of the page. Put them in a pile.

2. Cut out the game boards on the next page.

3. Take turns drawing cards.

4. If you have the figure that the card describes on your gameboard, cover it.

5. The first one to get three in a row, wins.

cube	point	angle	cylinder	rectangular prism
line	square	cone	circle	sphere
triangle	segment	rectangle	tangram	ray

Page is blank for cutting exercise on previous page.

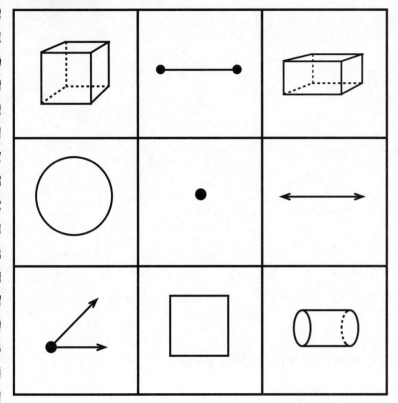

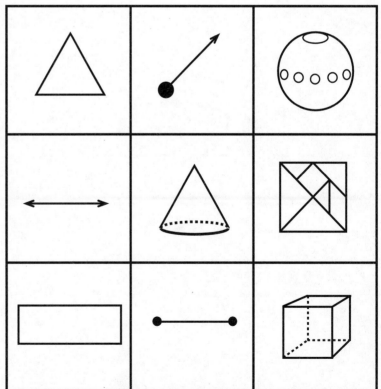

Page is blank for cutting exercise on previous page.

Name: _____

Geometry: Perimeter

The perimeter is the distance around an object. Find the perimeter by adding the lengths of all the sides.

Directions: Find the perimeter for each object (ft. = feet).

2 ft.

3 ft.　　　　3 ft.

2 ft.

6 ft.

6 ft.　　　　6 ft.

6 ft.　　　　6 ft.

6 ft.

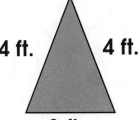

4 ft.　　　4 ft.

3 ft.

10 ft.
_____

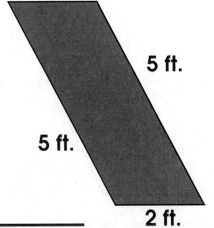

2 ft.

5 ft.

5 ft.

2 ft.
_____

10 ft.

3 ft.　　　　　　　　　　3 ft.

10 ft.

_____

1 ft.

1 ft.　　1 ft.

1 ft.　　　1 ft.

1 ft.　　1 ft.

1 ft.

_____

7 ft.　　5 ft.

5 ft.

_____

1 ft.　　3 ft.　　1 ft.

5 ft.

_____

67

Geometric Coloring

Directions: Color the geometric shapes in the box below.

Name: _____

Flower Power

Directions: Count the flowers and answer the questions.

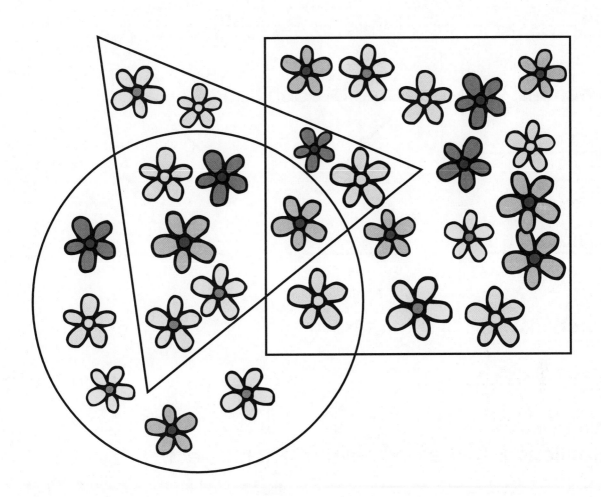

How many s are in the circle? _____

How many s are in the triangle? _____

How many s are in the square? _____

How many s in all? _____

Review

Directions: Write the decimal for each fraction.

$\frac{3}{10}$ = ____ $2\frac{4}{10}$ = ____ $12\frac{7}{10}$ = ____ $\frac{8}{10}$ = ____

Directions: Write the name of each figure.

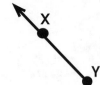
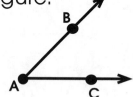
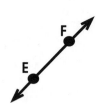

_____   _____   _____   _____

Directions: Add or subtract.

9.3 + 1.2 = ____   3.4 - 1.7 = ____   2.8 + 5.7 = ____

Directions: Find the perimeter of each object.

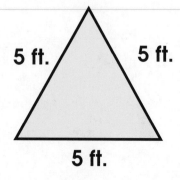
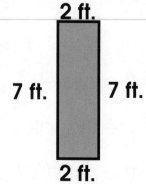
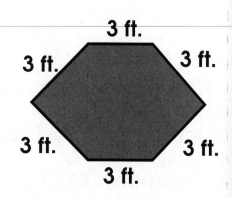

_____   _____   _____

Name: _____

Graphs

A graph is a drawing that shows information about numbers.

Directions: Color the picture. Then tell how many there are of each object by completing the graph.

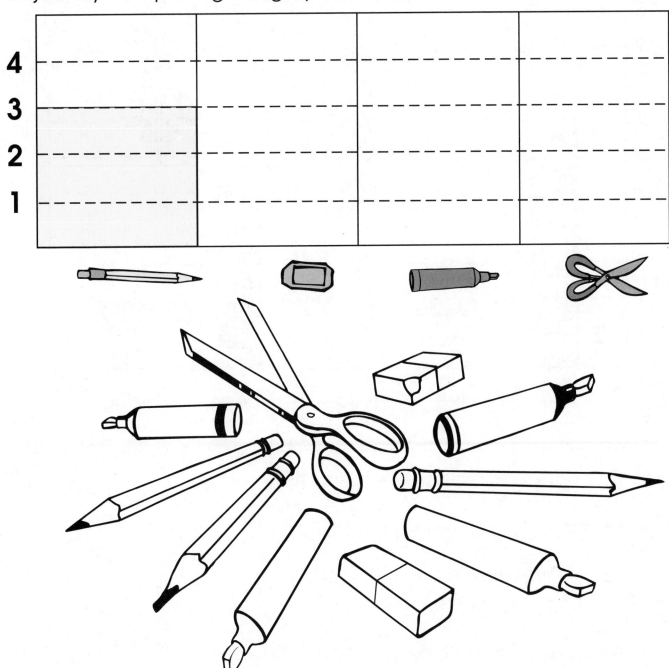

Name: _____

Graphs

Directions: Answer the questions about the graph.

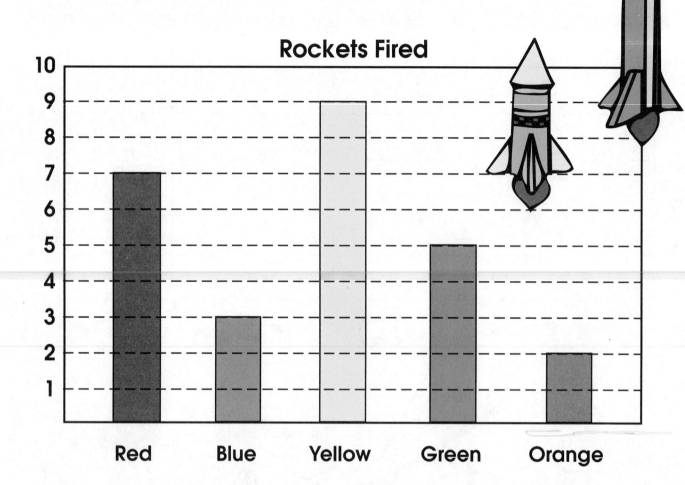

How many rockets did the Red Club fire? _____

How many rockets did the Green Club fire? _____

The Yellow Club fired 9 rockets. How many more rockets did it fire than the Blue Club? _____

How many rockets were fired in all? _____

Name: _____

Measurement: Inches

An inch is a unit of length in the standard measurement system.

Directions: Use a ruler to measure each object to the nearest $\frac{1}{4}$ inch. Write **in.** to stand for inch.

Example:

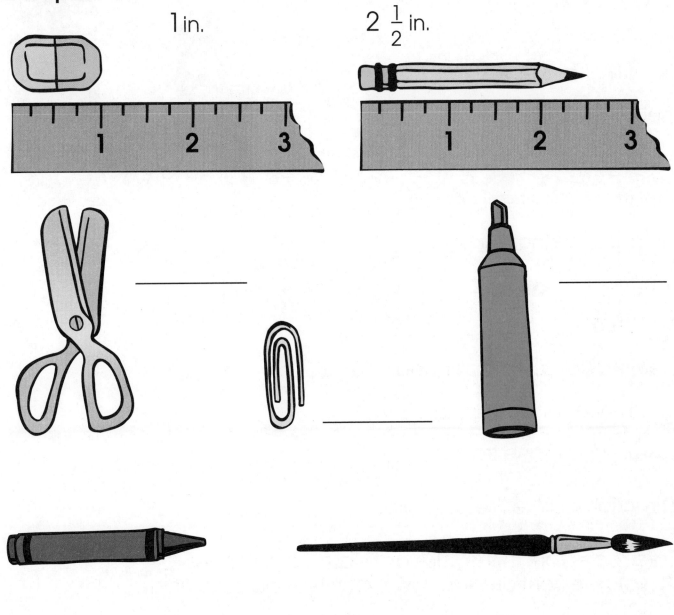

Name: _____

Measurement: Foot, Yard, Mile

Directions: Decide whether you would use foot, yard or mile to measure each object.

1 foot = 12 inches
1 yard = 36 inches or 3 feet
1 mile = 1,760 yards

length of a river ___miles___

height of a tree _____

width of a room _____

length of a football field _____

height of a door _____

length of a dress _____

length of a race _____

height of a basketball hoop _____

width of a window _____

distance a plane travels _____

Directions: Solve the problem.

Tara races Tom in the 100-yard dash. Tara finishes
10 yards in front of Tom. How many feet did Tara finish
in front of Tom?

_____

Name: _____

Measurement: Ounce and Pound

Ounces and pounds are measurements of weight in the standard measurement system. The ounce is used to measure the weight of very light objects. The pound is used to measure the weight of heavier objects. 16 ounces = 1 pound.

Example:

8 ounces   15 pounds

Directions: Decide if you would use ounces or pounds to measure the weight of each object. Circle your answer.

ounce   pound

ounce   pound

ounce   pound

ounce   pound

a chair: ounce   pound   **a table**:   ounce   pound

a shoe: ounce   pound   **a shirt**:   ounce   pound

Name:_____

Measurement: Centimeter

A centimeter is a unit of length in the metric system. There are 2.54 centimeters in an inch.

Directions: Use a centimeter ruler to measure each object to the nearest half of a centimeter. Write **cm**. to stand for centimeter.

Example:

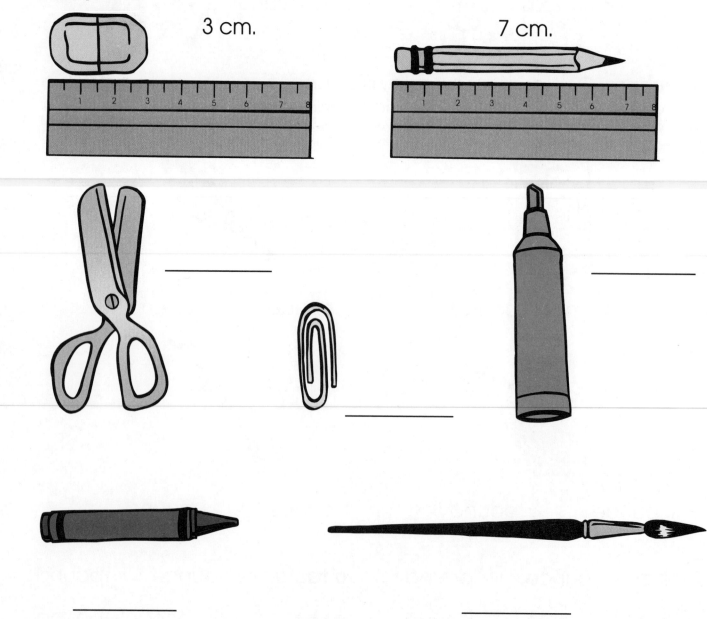

Measurement: Meter and Kilometer

Meters and kilometers are units of length in the metric system. A meter is equal to 39.37 inches. A kilometer is equal to about of $\frac{5}{8}$ a mile.

Directions: Decide whether you would use meter or kilometer to measure each object.

1 meter = 100 centimeters
1 kilometer = 1,000 meters

length of a river ___kilometer___

height of a tree _____

width of a room _____

length of a football field _____

height of a door _____

length of a dress _____

length of a race _____

height of a basketball pole _____

width of a window _____

distance a plane travels _____

Directions: Solve the problem.

Tara races Tom in the 100-meter dash. Tara finishes 10 meters in front of Tom. How many centimeters did Tara finish in front of Tom?

_____

Review

Directions: Circle the correct answers.

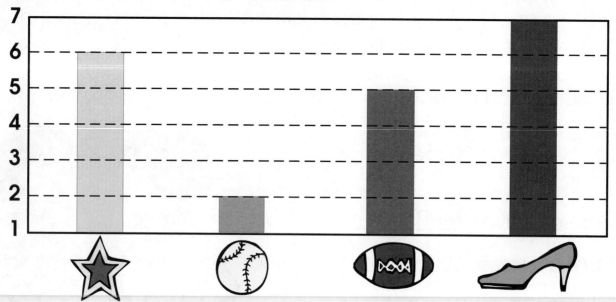

Are there more shoes or stars?	stars	shoes
How many more footballs than baseballs?	2	3
Are there fewer stars or footballs?	stars	footballs

Which would you use to measure...

...a horse?	ounce	pound
...a bird?	ounce	pound
...length of a car?	inches	feet
...width of a river?	inches	yards
...height of a room?	centimeters	meters
...length of a river?	meters	kilometers

Coordinates

Directions: Locate the points on the grid and color in each box.

What animal did you form?_____

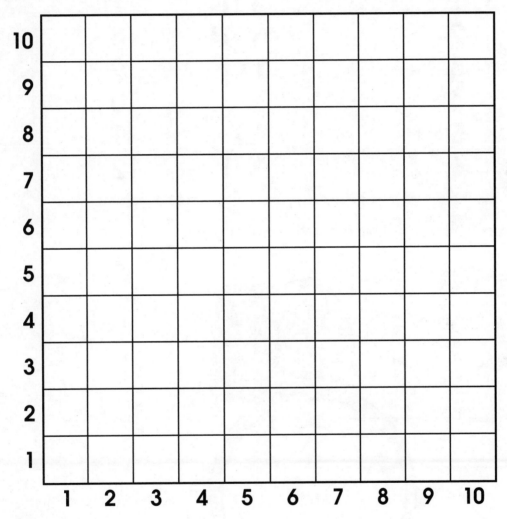

(across, up)

(4, 7)	(4, 1)	(7, 1)	(3, 5)	(2, 8)	(8, 6)	(4, 8)	(3, 7)
(5, 4)	(6, 5)	(5, 5)	(6, 6)	(7, 3)	(8, 5)	(10, 5)	(4, 3)
(7, 6)	(4, 6)	(1, 8)	(6, 4)	(7, 2)	(4, 5)	(9, 6)	(4, 9)
(3, 6)	(7, 5)	(5, 6)	(4, 2)	(4, 4)	(7, 4)	(2, 7)	(3, 8)

Name: _____

Roman Numerals

Another way to write numbers is to use Roman numerals.

I	1	VII	7
II	2	VIII	8
III	3	IX	9
IV	4	X	10
V	5	XI	11
VI	6	XII	12

Directions: Fill in the Roman numerals on the watch.

What time is it on the watch?

_____ o'clock

Roman Numerals

I	1	VII	7
II	2	VIII	8
III	3	IX	9
IV	4	X	10
V	5	XI	11
VI	6	XII	12

Directions: Write the number.

V _____   VII _____

X _____   IX _____

II _____   XII _____

Directions: Write the Roman numeral.

4 _____   5 _____

10 _____   8 _____

6 _____   3 _____

Time: Hour, Half-Hour, Quarter-Hour, 5 Min. Intervals

Directions: Write the time shown on each clock.

Example:

7:15

7:00

Name: _____

Time: a.m. and p.m.

In telling time, the hours between 12:00 midnight and 12:00 noon are a.m. hours. The hours between 12:00 noon and 12:00 midnight are p.m. hours.

Directions: Draw a line between the times that are the same.

Example:

7:30 in the morning   7:30 a.m.
half-past seven a.m.
seven thirty in the morning

9:00 in the evening   9:00 p.m.
nine o'clock at night

six o'clock in the evening   8:00 a.m.

3:30 a.m.   six o'clock in the morning

4:15 p.m.   6:00 p.m.

eight o'clock in the morning   eleven o'clock in the evening

quarter past five in the evening   three thirty in the morning

11:00 p.m.   four fifteen in the evening

6:00 a.m.   5:15 p.m.

Time: Minutes

A minute is a measurement of time. There are sixty seconds in a minute and sixty minutes in an hour.

Directions: Write the time shown on each clock.

Example:

Each mark is one minute.
The hand is at mark number 6.

Write: 5:06
Read: six minutes after five.

_____

_____

_____

_____

_____

_____

_____

_____

_____

_____

_____

_____

Time: Addition

Directions: Add the hours and minutes together.
(Remember, 1 hour equals 60 minutes.)

Example:

```
  2 hours 10 minutes
+ 1 hour  50 minutes
  3 hours 60 minutes
         (1 hour)
  4 hours
```

```
  4 hours 20 minutes
+ 2 hours 10 minutes
  6 hours 30 minutes
```

```
  9 hours
+ 2 hours
```

```
  1 hour
+ 5 hours
```

```
  6 hours
+ 3 hours
```

```
  6 hours 15 minutes
+ 1 hour  15 minutes
```

```
  10 hours 30 minutes
+  1 hour  10 minutes
```

```
  3 hours 40 minutes
+ 8 hours 20 minutes
```

```
  11 hours 15 minutes
+  1 hour  30 minutes
```

```
  4 hours 15 minutes
+ 5 hours 45 minutes
```

```
  7 hours 10 minutes
+ 1 hour  30 minutes
```

Name: _____

Time: Subtraction

Directions: Subtract the hours and minutes.
(Remember, 1 hour equals 60 minutes.)
"Borrow" from the "hours" if you need to.

Example:

$$
\begin{array}{l}
\quad 5 \qquad 70 \\
\cancel{6} \text{ hours } \cancel{10} \text{ minutes} \\
- 2 \text{ hours } 30 \text{ minutes} \\
\hline
\;\; 3 \text{ hours } 40 \text{ minutes}
\end{array}
$$

12 hours
- 2 hours

5 hour
- 3 hours

2 hours
- 1 hour

5 hours 30 minutes
- 2 hours 15 minutes

9 hours 45 minutes
- 3 hours 15 minutes

11 hours 50 minutes
- 4 hours 35 minutes

12 hours
- 6 hours 30 minutes

7 hours 15 minutes
- 5 hours 30 minutes

8 hours 10 minutes
- 4 hours 40 minutes

Money: Coins and Dollars

 penny =
1¢ or $.01

 nickel =
5¢ or $.05

 dime =
10¢ or $.10

 quarter =
25¢ or $.25

 half-dollar =
50¢ or $.50

dollar = 100¢ or $1.00

Directions: Write the amount for each group of money shown. Use a dollar sign and decimal point. The first one is done for you.

$.07

_____

_____

_____

_____

_____

Money: Five-Dollar Bill and Ten-Dollar Bill

Directions: Write the amount for each group of money shown. Use a dollar sign and decimal point. The first one is done for you.

Five-dollar bill =
5 one dollar bills

Ten-dollar bill =
2 five-dollar bills or
10 one-dollar bills

$15.00   _____

_____   _____

7 one-dollar bills, 2 quarters _____

2 five-dollar bills, 3 one-dollar bills, half-dollar _____

3 ten-dollar bills, 1 five-dollar bill, 3 quarters _____

Money: Counting Change

Directions: Subtract the money using decimals to show how much change a person would receive in each of the following.

Example:

Bill had 3 dollars.
He bought a baseball for $2.83.
How much change did he receive?

$3.00
-$2.83
$ .17

Paid 2 dollars.

_____

Paid 1 dollar.

_____

Paid 5 dollars.

_____

Paid 10 dollars.

_____

Paid 4 dollars.

_____

Paid 7 dollars.

_____

Money: Comparing

Directions: Compare the amount of money in the left column with the price of the object in the right column. Is the amount of money in the left column enough to purchase the object in the right column? Circle yes or no.

Example:

Alice has 2 dollars. She wants to buy a CD for $1.75. Does she have enough money?

(Yes) No

      Yes No

      Yes No

      Yes No

Review

Directions: Complete each clock to show the time written below it.

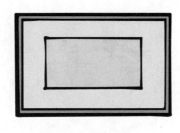

7:15   3:07   6:25

Directions: Write the time using a.m. or p.m.

seven twenty-two in the evening _____

three fifteen in the morning _____

eight thirty at night _____

Directions: Write the correct amount of money.

_____   _____

Joey paid $4.67 for a model
car. He gave the clerk a five-
dollar bill. How much change
should he receive?

_____

Name: _____

Problem-Solving: Addition, Subtraction

Directions: Read and solve each problem. The first one is done for you.

The clown started the day with 200 balloons. He gave away 128 of them. Some broke. At the end of the day he had 18 balloons left. How many of the balloons broke?   **54**

On Monday, there were 925 tickets sold to adults and 1,412 tickets sold to children. How many more children attended the fair than adults?   _____

At one game booth, prizes were given out for scoring 500 points in three attempts. Sally scored 178 points on her first attempt, 149 points on her second attempt and 233 points on her third attempt. Did Sally win a prize?   _____

The prize-winning steer weighed 2,348 pounds. The runner-up steer weighed 2,179 pounds. How much more did the prize steer weigh?   _____

There were 3,418 people at the fair on Tuesday, and 2,294 people on Wednesday. What was the total number of people there for the two days?   _____

Problem-Solving: Multiplication, Division

Directions: Read and solve each problem.

Jeff and Terry are planting a garden. They plant 3 rows of green beans with 8 plants in each row. How many green bean plants are there in the garden?   _____

There are 45 tomato plants in the garden. There are 5 rows of them. How many tomato plants are in each row?   _____

The children have 12 plants each of lettuce, broccoli and spinach. How many plants are there in all?   _____

Jeff planted 3 times as many cucumber plants as Terry. He planted 15 of them. How many did Terry plant?   _____

Terry planted 12 pepper plants. He planted twice as many green pepper plants as red pepper plants. How many green pepper plants are there?   _____

How many red pepper plants?   _____

Name:_____

Problem-Solving: Fractions, Decimals

A fraction is a number that names part of a whole, such as $\frac{1}{2}$ or $\frac{1}{3}$.

Directions: Read and solve each problem.

There are 20 large animals on the Browns' farm. Two-fifths are horses, two-fifths are cows and the rest are pigs. Are there more pigs or cows on the farm? _____

Farmer Brown had 40 eggs to sell. He sold half of them in the morning. In the afternoon, he sold half of what was left. How many eggs did Farmer Brown have at the end of the day? _____

There is a fence running around seven-tenths of the farm. How much of the farm does not have a fence around it? Write the amount as a decimal. _____

The Browns have 10 chickens. Two are roosters and the rest are hens. Write a decimal for the number that are roosters and for the number that are hens. _____ roosters _____ hens

Mrs. Brown spends three-fourths of her day working outside and the rest working inside. Does she spend more time inside or outside? _____

Name: _____

Problem-Solving: Measurement

Directions: Read and solve each problem.

This year, hundreds of people ran in the
Capital City Marathon. The race is 4.2 kilometers
long. When the first person crossed the finish
line, the last person was at the 3.7 kilometer point.
How far ahead was the winner?   _____

Dennis crossed the finish line 10 meters ahead of Lucy.
Lucy was 5 meters ahead of Sam. How far ahead of Sam
was Dennis?   _____

Tony ran 320 yards from school to his home. Then he ran
290 yards to Jay's house. Together Tony and Jay ran 545
yards to the store. How many yards in all did Tony run?   _____

The teacher measured the heights of three children in her
class. Marsha was 51 inches tall, Jimmy was 48 inches tall
and Ted was $52\frac{1}{2}$ inches tall. How much taller is Ted than
Marsha?   _____

How much taller is he than Jimmy?   _____

Name:_____

Problem-Solving: Measurement

Directions: Read and solve each problem.

Ralph has $8.75. He buys a teddy bear and a puzzle.
How much money does he have left?   _____

Kelly wants to buy a teddy bear and a ball. She has $7.25.
How much more money does she need?   _____

Kim paid a five-dollar bill, two one-dollar bills, two quarters,
one dime and eight pennies for a book.
How much did it cost?   _____

Michelle leaves for school at 7:45 a.m.
It takes her 20 minutes to get there.
On the clock, draw the time that she
arrives at school.

Frank takes piano lessons every
Saturday morning at 11:30.
The lesson lasts for an hour and
15 minutes. On the clock, draw
the time his piano lesson ends.
Is it a.m. or p.m.?
Circle the correct answer.

Name: _____

Review

Directions: Read and solve each of the problems.

The baker sets out 9 baking pans with 6 rolls on each one. How many rolls are there in all? _____

A dozen brownies cost $1.29. James pays for a dozen brownies with a five-dollar bill. How much change does he receive? _____

Theresa has four quarters, a nickel and three pennies. How much more money does she need to buy brownies? _____

The baker made 24 loaves of bread. At the end of the day, he has one-fourth left. How many did he sell? _____

Two loaves of bread weigh a pound. How many loaves are needed to make five pounds? _____

The bakery opens at 8:30 a.m. It closes nine and a half hours later. What time does it close? _____

Math Terms Crossword

Directions: Use your glossary to help you fill in the words.

Math Terms Crossword Clues

Across

1. 100¢

3. Symbols used to write numbers

6. A measurement of distance in the standard measurement system

7. Part of a line with 2 end points

8. A measurement of distance in the metric system

10. A figure with 4 corners and 4 sides

12. Answer in a subtraction problem

13. Smaller number that is divided into the dividend

14. Answer of a division problem

17. A measurement of weight in the standard measurement system

18. A measurement of distance in the standard measurement system

19. Answer in a multiplication problem

21. 2 rays with the same end point

22. Putting together 2 or more numbers to find the sum

23. A drawing that shows information about numbers

Down

1. Operation to find out how many times one number is contained in another

2. A number multiplied together in a problem

3. A number with one or more places to the right

4. A figure with 3 corners and 3 sides

5. A measurement of length in the metric system

9. A short way to find the sum of adding the same number many times

11. A point at the end of a line segment or ray

15. The number left over in the quotient

16. A number that names part of a whole

19. Distance around an object

20. A figure with 4 corners and 4 side of equal length

Challenge

Directions: See how many words you can make from the letters in the word "Mathematics."

MATHEMATICS

_____   _____

_____   _____

_____   _____

_____   _____

_____   _____

_____   _____

For a challenge, time yourself or race another person.

Review

Place Value

Directions: Write the number's value in each place: **678,421**.

_____ ones   _____ hundred thousands

_____ thousands   _____ hundreds

_____ tens   _____ ten thousands

Addition and Subtraction

Directions: Add or subtract. Remember to regroup, if you need to.

$$\begin{array}{r} 88 \\ -\ 19 \\ \hline \end{array} \qquad \begin{array}{r} 46 \\ +\ 39 \\ \hline \end{array} \qquad \begin{array}{r} 75 \\ +\ 24 \\ \hline \end{array} \qquad \begin{array}{r} 93 \\ -\ 68 \\ \hline \end{array} \qquad \begin{array}{r} 76 \\ -\ 59 \\ \hline \end{array}$$

$$\begin{array}{r} 683 \\ -\ 496 \\ \hline \end{array} \qquad \begin{array}{r} 855 \\ +\ 138 \\ \hline \end{array} \qquad \begin{array}{r} 84 \\ 49 \\ +\ 62 \\ \hline \end{array} \qquad \begin{array}{r} 97 \\ 54 \\ +\ 361 \\ \hline \end{array} \qquad \begin{array}{r} 9,731 \\ -\ 4,664 \\ \hline \end{array}$$

Rounding

Directions: Round to the nearest 10, 100 or 1,000.

72 _____   49 _____   31 _____   66 _____

151 _____   296 _____   917 _____   621 _____

Multiplication and Division

$$3 \times 6$$ $$3 \times 8$$ $$9 \times 8$$ $$9 \times 5$$ $$7 \times 2$$

$$5\overline{)25}$$ $$2\overline{)6}$$ $$3\overline{)18}$$ $$8\overline{)24}$$ $$7\overline{)49}$$

Fractions

$\frac{1}{3}$ of 12 = _____

$\frac{1}{7}$ of 28 = _____

$\frac{1}{9}$ of 45 = _____

Directions: Color parts to match the fractions given.

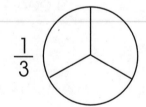

$\frac{1}{3}$

$\frac{2}{4}$

$\frac{2}{6}$

Decimals

Directions: Write the decimal for each fraction.

$\frac{4}{10}$ = _____ $3\frac{3}{10}$ = _____ $\frac{9}{10}$ = _____ $21\frac{3}{10}$ = _____

Directions: Add or Subtract.

8.2 + 1.1 = _____   3.6 - 1.8 = _____   3.9 + 2.6 = _____

Geometry

Directions: Write the name for each figure.

_____   _____   _____   _____

Directions: Find the perimeter of each object.

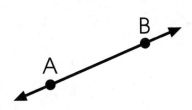   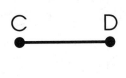   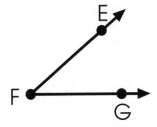

_____   _____   _____

Name: _____

Graphing

Directions: Answer the questions.

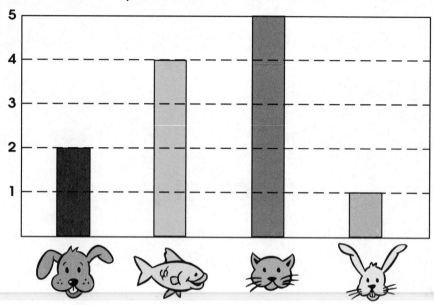

Which animal is there the most of?   _____

Which animal is there the fewest of?   _____

How many animals altogether?   _____

Measurements

Directions: Answer the questions.
What unit of measure would you use to measure...

Example: ...a cow?   _pound_

...a mouse?   _____

...length of a pencil?   _____

...length of a semi-truck?   _____

...length of a river?   _____

...width of a river?   _____

...height of a flag pole?   _____

Time

Directions: Complete each clock to show the time written below it.

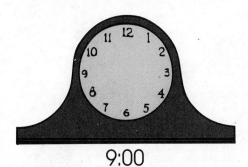

9:00

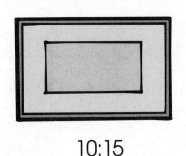

10:15

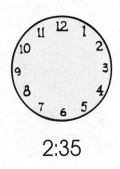

2:35

Directions: Write the time, using a.m. or p.m.

six twenty-two in the evening _____

nine forty-six in the morning _____

Directions: Add.

$$\begin{array}{r} 2 \text{ hours } 15 \text{ minutes} \\ + 4 \text{ hours } 30 \text{ minutes} \\ \hline \end{array}$$

$$\begin{array}{r} 1 \text{ hour } 30 \text{ minutes} \\ + 4 \text{ hours } 30 \text{ minutes} \\ \hline \end{array}$$

$$\begin{array}{r} 12 \text{ hours } 45 \text{ minutes} \\ - 4 \text{ hours } 30 \text{ minutes} \\ \hline \end{array}$$

$$\begin{array}{r} 8 \text{ hours } 30 \text{ minutes} \\ - 3 \text{ hours } 45 \text{ minutes} \\ \hline \end{array}$$

Name: _____

Money

Directions: Write the amount of money.

_____   _____

$$\begin{array}{r} \$5.00 \\ -\ 4.67 \\ \hline \end{array}$$ $$\begin{array}{r} \$6.51 \\ -\ 2.49 \\ \hline \end{array}$$

Problem-Solving

Katarina has 12 pieces of cake. After school, she has $\frac{1}{4}$ of the cake left. How much cake was eaten?

_____

4 jars of play dough weigh 1 pound. How many jars would weigh 3 pounds?

_____

Glossary

Addition: "Putting together" or adding two or more numbers to find the sum.

Angle: Two rays with the same end point.

Centimeter: A measurement of length in the metric system. There are 2.54 centimeters in an inch.

Decimal: A number with one or more places to the right of a decimal point, such as 6.5 or 3.78. Money amounts are written with two places to the right of a decimal point, such as $1.30.

Difference: The answer in a subtraction problem.

Digit: The symbols used to write numbers: 0, 1, 2, 3, 4, 5, 6, 7, 8 and 9.

Dividend: The larger number that is divided by the smaller number, or divisor, in a division problem. In the problem $28 \div 7 = 4$, 28 is the dividend.

Division: An operation to find out how many times one number is contained in another number. For example, $28 \div 4 = 7$ means that there are seven groups of four in 28.

Divisor: The smaller number that is divided into the dividend in a division problem. In the problem $28 \div 7 = 4$, 7 is the divisor.

Dollar: A dollar is equal to one hundred cents. It is written $1.00.

End Point: A point at the end of a line segment or ray.

Factors: The numbers multiplied together in a multiplication problem.

Fraction: A number that names part of a whole, such as $\frac{1}{2}$ or $\frac{1}{3}$.

Geometry: The branch of mathematics that has to do with points, lines and shapes.

Graph: A drawing that shows information about numbers.

Kilometer: A measurement of distance in the metric system. There are 1,000 meters in a kilometer.

Meter: A measurement of length in the metric system. A meter is equal to 39.37 inches.

Mile: A measurement of distance in the standard measurement system. A mile is equal to 1,760 yards.

Multiplication: A short way to find the sum of adding the same number a certain amount of times. For example, $7 \times 4 = 28$ instead of $7 + 7 + 7 + 7 = 28$.

Ounce: A measurement of weight in the standard measurement system. There are sixteen ounces in a pound.

Perimeter: The distance around an object. Find the perimeter by adding the lengths of the sides.

Place Value: The value of a digit, or numeral, shown by where it is in the number.

Product: The answer of a multiplication problem.

Quotient: The answer of a division problem.

Ray: A line segment with only one end point. It goes on and on in the other direction.

Rectangle: A figure with four corners and four sides. Sides opposite each other are the same length.

Regroup: To use ten ones to form one ten, ten tens to form 100 and so on.

Remainder: The number left over in the quotient of a division problem.

Segment: A part of a line with two end points.

Square: A figure with four corners and four sides of the same length.

Subtraction: "Taking away" or subtracting one number from another to find the difference.

Triangle: A figure with three corners and three sides.

Yard: A measurement of distance in the standard measurement system. There are three feet in a yard.

Answer Key

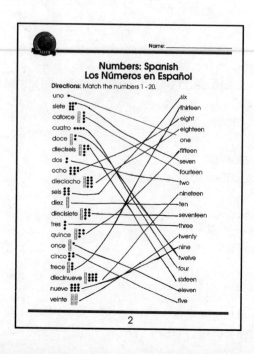

Numbers: Spanish
Los Números en Español

Directions: Match the numbers 1 - 20.

uno	six
siete	thirteen
catorce	eight
cuatro	eighteen
doce	one
dieciseis	fifteen
dos	seven
ocho	fourteen
dieciocho	two
seis	nineteen
diez	ten
diecisiete	seventeen
tres	three
quince	twenty
once	nine
cinco	twelve
trece	four
diecinueve	sixteen
nueve	eleven
veinte	five

2

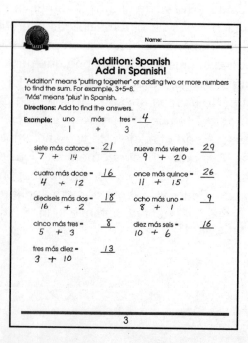

Addition: Spanish
Add in Spanish!

"Addition" means "putting together" or adding two or more numbers to find the sum. For example, 3+5=8.
"Más" means "plus" in Spanish.

Directions: Add to find the answers.

Example: uno   más   tres = _4_
              1   +   3

siete más catorce = _21_   nueve más viente = _29_
7 + 14   9 + 20

cuatro más doce = _16_   once más quince = _26_
4 + 12   11 + 15

dieciseis más dos = _18_   ocho más uno = _9_
16 + 2   8 + 1

cinco más tres = _8_   diez más seis = _16_
5 + 3   10 + 6

tres más diez = _13_
3 + 10

3

Panel 1 (page 4): Addition

Directions: Add.
Example:

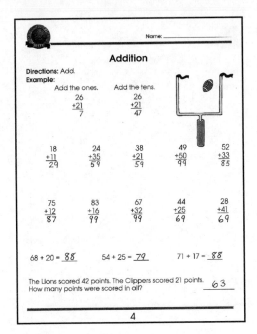

Add the ones.	Add the tens.
26 +21 7	26 +21 47

18 +11 29	24 +35 59	38 +21 59	49 +50 99	52 +33 85

75 +12 87	83 +16 99	67 +32 99	44 +25 69	28 +41 69

68 + 20 = __88__   54 + 25 = __79__   71 + 17 = __88__

The Lions scored 42 points. The Clippers scored 21 points. How many points were scored in all? __63__

4

Panel 2 (page 7): Place Value

The place value of a digit, or numeral, is shown by where it is in the number. For example, in the number 1,234, 1 has the place value of thousands, 2 is hundreds, 3 is tens and 4 is ones.

Hundred Thousands	Ten Thousands	Thousands	Hundreds	Tens	Ones
9	4	3	8	5	2

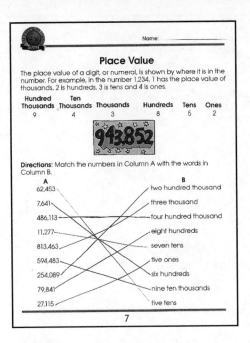

943,852

Directions: Match the numbers in Column A with the words in Column B.

A	B
62,453	two hundred thousand
7,641	three thousand
486,113	four hundred thousand
11,277	eight hundreds
813,463	seven tens
594,483	five ones
254,089	six hundreds
79,841	nine ten thousands
27,115	five tens

7

Panel 3 (page 5): Addition: Football Math

Directions: Follow the plays of your favorite team.

A touchdown is worth 6 points.
A field goal is worth 3 points.

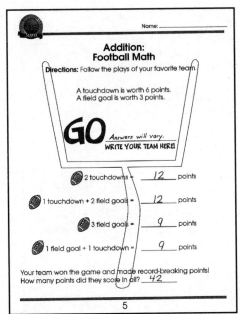

GO — *Answers will vary.*
WRITE YOUR TEAM HERE!

2 touchdowns = __12__ points

1 touchdown + 2 field goals = __12__ points

3 field goals = __9__ points

1 field goal + 1 touchdown = __9__ points

Your team won the game and made record-breaking points! How many points did they score in all? __42__

5

Panel 4 (page 8): Place Value

Directions: Use the code to color the rings.
If the number has:
7 ten thousands, color it red.
1 thousand, color it blue.
4 hundred thousands, color it green.
6 tens, color it brown.
8 ones, color it yellow.

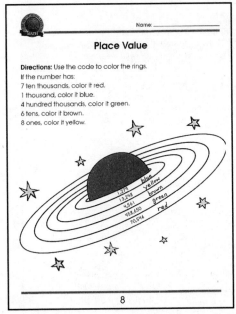

1,274 — blue
13,248 — yellow
4,561 — brown
456,650 — green
70,596 — red

8

Panel 5 (page 6): Subtraction

Subtraction means "taking away" or subtracting one number from another to find the difference. For example, 10 - 3 = 7.
Directions: Subtract.
Example:

Subtract the ones.	Subtract the tens.
39 -24 5	39 -24 15

48 -35 13	95 -22 73	87 -16 71	55 -43 12

37 -14 23	69 -57 12	44 -23 21	99 -78 21

66 - 44 = __22__   57 - 33 = __24__

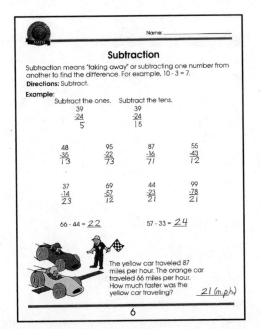

The yellow car traveled 87 miles per hour. The orange car traveled 66 miles per hour. How much faster was the yellow car traveling? __21 (m.p.h.)__

6

Panel 6 (page 9): Addition: Regrouping

Addition means "putting together" or adding two or more numbers to find the sum. For example, 3 + 5 = 8. To regroup is to use ten ones to form one ten, ten tens to form one 100 and so on.

Directions: Add using regrouping.
Example:

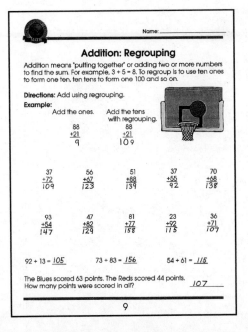

Add the ones.	Add the tens with regrouping.
88 +21 9	88 +21 109

37 +72 109	56 +67 123	51 +88 139	37 +55 92	70 +68 138

93 +54 147	47 +82 129	81 +77 158	23 +92 115	36 +71 107

92 + 13 = __105__   73 + 83 = __156__   54 + 61 = __115__

The Blues scored 63 points. The Reds scored 44 points. How many points were scored in all? __107__

9

Subtraction: Regrouping

Subtraction means "taking away" or subtracting one number from another to find the difference. For example, 10 - 3 = 7. To regroup is to use one ten to form ten ones, one 100 to form ten tens and so on.

Directions: Study the example. Subtract using regrouping.

Example:

$$
\begin{array}{rcl}
32 &=& 2\ tens + 12\ ones \\
-13 &=& 1\ ten + \underline{3\ ones} \\
\hline
19 &=& 1\ ten + 9\ ones
\end{array}
$$

33 -28 5	86 -59 27	92 -37 55	71 -48 23
63 -47 16	45 -18 27	31 -22 9	55 -39 16

82 - 69 = __13__   73 - 36 = __37__

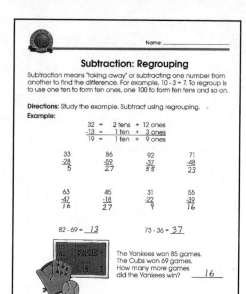

The Yankees won 85 games. The Cubs won 69 games. How many more games did the Yankees win? __16__

10

Addition: Regrouping

Directions: Study the example. Add using regrouping.

Examples:

Add the ones. Regroup.		Add the tens. Regroup.		Add the hundreds.
1 156 +267 3	6 +7 13	11 5 +6 12	1 156 +267 23	1 156 +267 423

29 46 +12 87	81 78 +33 192	52 67 +23 142	49 37 +19 105	162 +349 511
273 +198 471	655 +297 952	783 +148 931	385 +169 554	428 +122 550

Sally went bowling. She had scores of 115, 129 and 103. What was her total score for three games? __347__

13

Addition And Subtraction: Regrouping

Addition means "putting together" or adding two or more numbers to find the sum. Subtraction means "taking away" or subtracting one number from another to find the difference. To regroup is to use one ten to form ten ones, one 100 to form ten tens and so on.

Directions: Add or subtract. Regroup when needed.

92 -47 45	58 +26 84	63 +18 81	77 -38 39
27 -17 10	31 +42 73	56 -29 27	67 +33 100
72 +19 91	87 -58 29	93 -89 4	54 +27 81

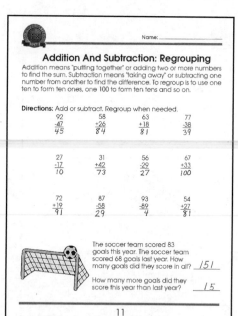

The soccer team scored 83 goals this year. The soccer team scored 68 goals last year. How many goals did they score in all? __151__

How many more goals did they score this year than last year? __15__

11

Addition: Regrouping

Directions: Add using regrouping. Then use the code to discover the name of a United States president.

348 +752 1,100	642 +277 919	386 +787 1,173	184 +875 1,059	578 +874 1,452
653 +768 1,421	653 +359 1,012	946 +239 1,185	393 +257 650	199 +843 1,042
721 +679 1,400				

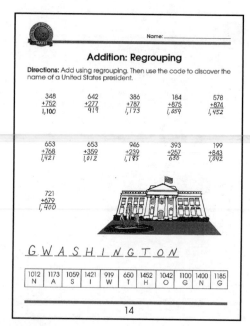

G W A S H I N G T O N

1012	1173	1059	1421	919	650	1452	1042	1100	1400	1185
N	A	S	I	W	T	H	O	G	N	G

14

Review

Directions: Write this number on the blank:

4 hundred thousands
5 ten thousands
1 thousand
8 hundreds
3 tens
3 ones

__4 5 1 , 8 3 3__

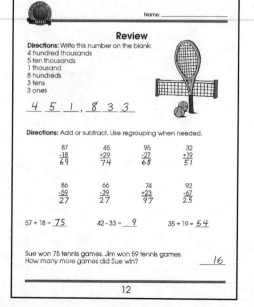

Directions: Add or subtract. Use regrouping when needed.

87 -18 69	45 +29 74	95 -27 68	32 +19 51
86 -59 27	66 -39 27	74 +23 97	92 -67 25

57 + 18 = __75__   42 - 33 = __9__   35 + 19 = __54__

Sue won 75 tennis games. Jim won 59 tennis games. How many more games did Sue win? __16__

12

Addition: Regrouping

Directions: Study the example. Add using regrouping.

Example

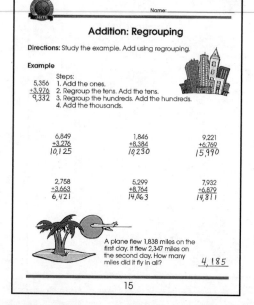

5,356   Steps:
+3,976   1. Add the ones.
9,332   2. Regroup the tens. Add the tens.
         3. Regroup the hundreds. Add the hundreds.
         4. Add the thousands.

6,849 +3,276 10,125	1,846 +8,384 10,230	9,221 +6,769 15,990
2,758 +3,663 6,421	5,299 +8,764 14,063	7,932 +6,879 14,811

A plane flew 1,838 miles on the first day. It flew 2,347 miles on the second day. How many miles did it fly in all? __4,185__

15

Addition: Mental Math

Directions: Try to do these addition problems in your head without using paper and pencil.

7 +4 = 11	6 +3 = 9	8 +1 = 9	10 + 2 = 12	2 +9 = 11	6 +6 = 12
10 +20 = 30	40 +20 = 60	80 +100 = 180	60 +30 = 90	50 +70 = 120	100 + 40 = 140
350 +150 = 500	300 +500 = 800	400 +800 = 1,200	450 + 10 = 460	680 +100 = 780	900 + 70 = 970
1,000 + 200 = 1,200	4,000 400 + 30 = 4,430	300 200 + 80 = 580	8,000 500 + 60 = 8,560	9,800 + 150 = 9,950	7,000 300 + 30 = 7,330

16

Subtraction: Regrouping

Directions: Study the example. Follow the steps. Subtract using regrouping. If you have to regroup to subtract ones and there are no tens, you must regroup twice.

Example:

300
-182
118

Steps:
1. Subtract ones. You cannot subtract 2 ones from 0 ones.
2. Regroup. No tens. Regroup hundreds (2 hundreds + 10 tens).
3. Regroup tens (9 tens + 10 ones).
4. Subtract 2 ones from ten ones.
5. Subtract 8 tens from 9 tens.
6. Subtract 1 hundred from 2 hundreds.

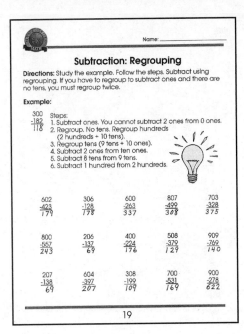

602 -423 = 179	306 -128 = 178	600 -263 = 337	807 -499 = 308	703 -328 = 375
800 -557 = 243	206 -137 = 69	400 -224 = 176	508 -379 = 129	909 -769 = 140
207 -138 = 69	604 -397 = 207	308 -199 = 109	700 -531 = 169	900 -278 = 622

19

Subtraction: Regrouping

Directions: Regrouping for subtraction is the opposite of regrouping for addition. Study the example. Subtract using regrouping. Then use the code to color the flowers.

Example:

647
-453
194

Steps:
1. Subtract ones.
2. Subtract tens. Five tens cannot be subtracted from 4 tens.
3. Regroup tens by regrouping 6 hundreds (5 hundreds + 10 tens).
4. Add the 10 tens to the four tens.
5. Subtract 5 tens from 14 tens.
6. Subtract the hundreds.

If the answer has:
1 one, color it red;
8 ones, color it pink;
5 ones, color it yellow.

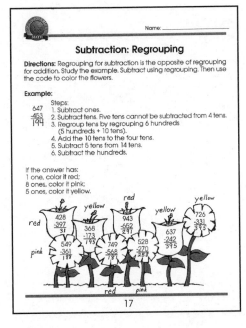

red 428 -397 = 31
yellow 368 -173 = 195
red 943 -652 = 291
yellow 637 -242 = 395
yellow 726 -331 = 395
pink 549 -361 = 188
749 -568 = 181
528 -270 = 257

17

Subtraction: Regrouping

Directions: Study the example. Follow the steps. Subtract using regrouping.

Example:

634
-455
179

Steps:
1. Subtract ones. You cannot subtract five ones from 4 ones.
2. Regroup ones by regrouping 3 tens to 2 tens + 10 ones.
3. Subtract 5 ones from 14 ones.
4. Regroup tens by regrouping hundreds (5 hundreds + 10 tens).
5. Subtract 5 tens from 12 tens.
6. Subtract hundreds.

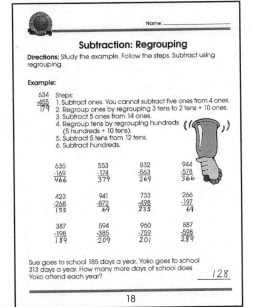

635 -169 = 466	553 -174 = 379	832 -563 = 269	944 -578 = 366
423 -268 = 155	941 -872 = 69	733 -498 = 235	266 -197 = 69
387 -198 = 189	594 -385 = 209	960 -759 = 201	887 -598 = 289

Sue goes to school 185 days a year. Yoko goes to school 313 days a year. How many more days of school does Yoko attend each year? _128_

18

Subtraction: Regrouping

Directions: Subtract. Regroup when necessary. The first one is done for you.

7,354 -5,295 = 2,059	4,214 -3,185 = 1,029	8,437 -5,338 = 3,099	6,837 -4,318 = 2,519
5,735 -3,826 = 1,909	1,036 - 947 = 89	6,735 -6,646 = 89	3,841 -1,953 = 1,888

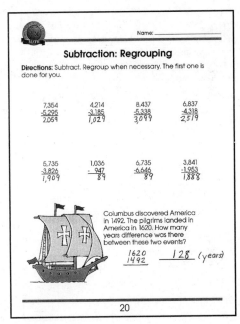

Columbus discovered America in 1492. The pilgrims landed in America in 1620. How many years difference was there between these two events?

1620
1492
_128_ (years)

20

Subtraction: Mental Math

Directions: Try to do these subtraction problems in your head without using paper and pencil.

9 -3 = 6	12 - 6 = 6	7 -6 = 1	5 -1 = 4	15 - 5 = 10	2 -0 = 2
40 -20 = 20	90 -80 = 10	100 - 50 = 50	20 -20 = 0	60 -10 = 50	70 -40 = 30
450 -250 = 200	500 -300 = 200	250 - 20 = 230	690 -100 = 590	320 - 20 = 300	900 -600 = 300
1,000 - 400 = 600	8,000 - 500 = 7,500	7,000 - 900 = 6,100	4,000 -2,000 = 2,000	9,500 -4,000 = 5,500	5,000 -2,000 = 3,000

21

111

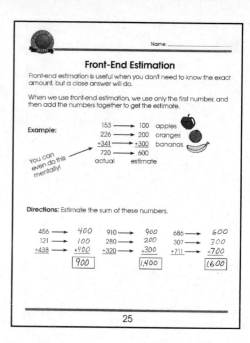

Review

Directions: Add or subtract using regrouping.

28	82	33	67
56	49	75	94
+93	+51	+128	+248
177	182	236	409

683	756	818	956
-495	+139	-387	+267
188	895	431	1,223

1,588	4,675	8,732	2,938
- 989	-2,976	-5,664	+3,459
599	1,699	3,068	6,397

To drive from New York City to Los Angeles is 2,832 miles. To drive from New York City to Miami is 1,327 miles. How much farther is it to drive from New York City to Los Angeles than from New York City to Miami?   **1,505**

2,832
- 1,327

22

Front-End Estimation

Front-end estimation is useful when you don't need to know the exact amount, but a close answer will do.

When we use front-end estimation, we use only the first number, and then add the numbers together to get the estimate.

Example:

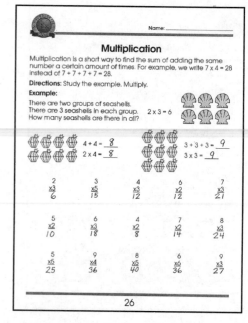

```
153  →  100   apples
226  →  200   oranges
+341 → +300   bananas
720     600
actual  estimate
```

You can even do this mentally!

Directions: Estimate the sum of these numbers.

456 →	400	910 →	900	686 →	600
121 →	100	280 →	200	307 →	300
+438 →	+400	+320 →	+300	+711 →	+700
	900		**1,400**		**1,600**

25

Rounding: The Nearest Ten

If the ones number is 5 or greater, "round up" to the nearest 10. If the ones number is 4 or less, the tens number stays the same and the ones number becomes a zero.

Examples: 15 round up to 20   23 round down to 20   47 round up to 50

7	10	58	60
12	10	81	80
33	30	94	90
27	30	44	40
73	70	88	90
25	30	66	70
39	40	70	70

23

Multiplication

Multiplication is a short way to find the sum of adding the same number a certain amount of times. For example, we write 7 x 4 = 28 instead of 7 + 7 + 7 + 7 = 28.

Directions: Study the example. Multiply.

Example:

There are two groups of seashells.
There are 3 seashells in each group.   2 x 3 = 6
How many seashells are there in all?

4 + 4 = **8**   3 + 3 + 3 = **9**
2 x 4 = **8**   3 x 3 = **9**

2	3	4	6	7
x3	x3	x3	x2	x3
6	15	12	12	21

5	6	4	7	8
x2	x3	x2	x2	x3
10	18	8	14	24

5	9	8	6	9
x5	x4	x5	x6	x3
25	36	40	36	27

26

Rounding: The Nearest Hundred

If the tens number is 5 or greater, "round up" to the nearest hundred. If the tens number is 4 or less, the hundreds number remains the same.

REMEMBER... Look at the number directly to the right of the place you are rounding to.

Example:

230 round down to 200   470 round up to 500

150 round up to 200   732 round down to 700

456	500	120	100
340	300	923	900
867	900	550	600
686	700	231	200
770	800	492	500

24

Multiplication

Directions: Multiply.

3	4	3
x5	x6	x8
15	24	24

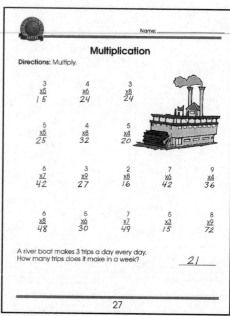

5	4	5
x5	x8	x4
25	32	20

6	3	2	7	9
x7	x9	x8	x6	x4
42	27	16	42	36

6	5	7	5	8
x8	x6	x7	x3	x9
48	30	49	15	72

A river boat makes 3 trips a day every day. How many trips does it make in a week?   **21**

27

Page 28 (top left)

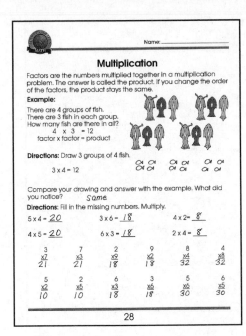

Multiplication

Factors are the numbers multiplied together in a multiplication problem. The answer is called the product. If you change the order of the factors, the product stays the same.

Example:

There are 4 groups of fish.
There are 3 fish in each group.
How many fish are there in all?
$$4 \times 3 = 12$$
factor x factor = product

Directions: Draw 3 groups of 4 fish.

$$3 \times 4 = 12$$

Compare your drawing and answer with the example. What did you notice? _Same_

Directions: Fill in the missing numbers. Multiply.

5 x 4 = _20_   3 x 6 = _18_   4 x 2 = _8_

4 x 5 = _20_   6 x 3 = _18_   2 x 4 = _8_

3	7	2	9	8	4
x7	x3	x9	x2	x4	x8
21	21	18	18	32	32

5	2	6	3	5	6
x2	x5	x3	x6	x6	x5
10	10	18	18	30	30

28

Page 29 (middle left)

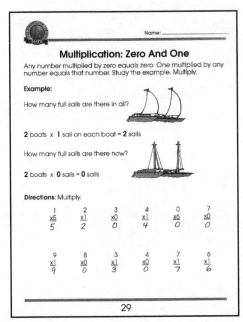

Multiplication: Zero And One

Any number multiplied by zero equals zero. One multiplied by any number equals that number. Study the example. Multiply.

Example:

How many full sails are there in all?

2 boats x **1** sail on each boat = **2** sails

How many full sails are there now?

2 boats x **0** sails = **0** sails

Directions: Multiply.

1	2	3	4	0	7
x5	x1	x0	x1	x6	x0
5	2	0	4	0	0

9	8	3	4	7	6
x1	x0	x1	x0	x1	x1
9	0	3	0	7	6

29

Page 30 (bottom left)

Multiplication

Directions: Time yourself as you multiply. How quickly can you complete this page?

3	8	1	1	3	0
x2	x7	x0	x6	x4	x4
6	56	0	6	12	0

4	4	2	9	9	5
x1	x4	x5	x3	x9	x3
4	16	10	27	81	15

0	2	9	8	7	4
x8	x6	x6	x5	x3	x2
0	12	54	40	21	8

3	2	4	1	0	3
x5	x0	x6	x3	x0	x3
15	0	24	3	0	9

30

Page 31 (top right)

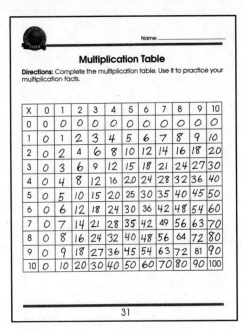

Multiplication Table

Directions: Complete the multiplication table. Use it to practice your multiplication facts.

X	0	1	2	3	4	5	6	7	8	9	10
0	0	0	0	0	0	0	0	0	0	0	0
1	0	1	2	3	4	5	6	7	8	9	10
2	0	2	4	6	8	10	12	14	16	18	20
3	0	3	6	9	12	15	18	21	24	27	30
4	0	4	8	12	16	20	24	28	32	36	40
5	0	5	10	15	20	25	30	35	40	45	50
6	0	6	12	18	24	30	36	42	48	54	60
7	0	7	14	21	28	35	42	49	56	63	70
8	0	8	16	24	32	40	48	56	64	72	80
9	0	9	18	27	36	45	54	63	72	81	90
10	0	10	20	30	40	50	60	70	80	90	100

31

Page 32 (middle right)

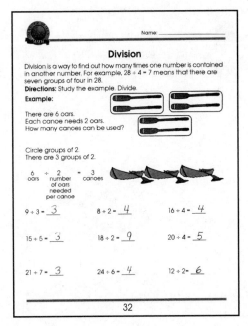

Division

Division is a way to find out how many times one number is contained in another number. For example, 28 ÷ 4 = 7 means that there are seven groups of four in 28.

Directions: Study the example. Divide.

Example:

There are 6 oars.
Each canoe needs 2 oars.
How many canoes can be used?

Circle groups of 2.
There are 3 groups of 2.

6	÷	2	=	3
oars		number of oars needed per canoe		canoes

9 ÷ 3 = _3_   8 ÷ 2 = _4_   16 ÷ 4 = _4_

15 ÷ 5 = _3_   18 ÷ 2 = _9_   20 ÷ 4 = _5_

21 ÷ 7 = _3_   24 ÷ 6 = _4_   12 ÷ 2 = _6_

32

Page 33 (bottom right)

Division

Directions: Divide. Draw a line from the boat to the sail with the correct answer.

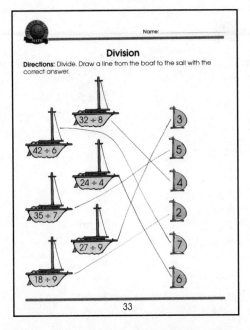

Boats	Sails
32 ÷ 8	3
42 ÷ 6	5
24 ÷ 4	4
35 ÷ 7	2
27 ÷ 9	7
18 ÷ 9	6

33

113

Order of Operations

When you solve a problem that involves more than one operation, this is the order to follow:

( )	Parentheses first
x	Multiplication
÷	Division
+	Addition
−	Subtraction

Example:
2 + (3 x 5) - 2 = 15
2 + 15 - 2 = 15
17 - 2 = 15

Directions: Solve the problems using the correct order of operations.

(5 - 3) + 4 x 7 = _30_
  2   28

1 + 2 x 3 + 4 = _11_
    6

6 x 3 - 1 = _17_
18

(8 ÷ 2) x 4 = _16_
  4

9 ÷ 3 x 3 + 0 = _1_
  9

5 - 2 + 2 = _5_
   3

34

Division

Division is a way to find out how many times one number is contained in another number. The ÷ sign means "divided by." Another way to divide is to use [. The dividend is the larger number that is divided by the smaller number, or divisor. The answer of a division problem is called the quotient.

Directions: Study the example. Divide.

Example:

20 ÷ 4 = 5
dividend divisor quotient

quotient
  5
4)20
divisor dividend

35 ÷ 7 = _5_   7)35 (5)   42 ÷ 6 = _7_   6)42 (7)

2)12 (6)   3)18 (6)   4)36 (9)   5)50 (10)

6)24 (4)   7)21 (3)   8)32 (4)   9)27 (3)

36 ÷ 6 = _6_   28 ÷ 4 = _7_   15 ÷ 5 = _3_   12 ÷ 2 = _6_

A tree farm has 36 trees. There are 4 rows of trees.
How many trees are there in each row?   _9_

37

Order of Operations

Directions: Use +, −, x and ÷ to complete the problems so the number sentence is true.

Example: 4 _+_ 2 _−_ 1 = 5

(8 _÷_ 2) _+_ 4 = 8

(1 _+_ 2) _÷_ 3 = 1

9 _+_ 3 _−_ 9 = 3

(7 _−_ 5) _X_ 1 = 2

8 _X_ 5 _÷_ 4 = 10

5 _−_ 4 _X_ 1 = 1

REMEMBER... USE THE ORDER OF OPERATIONS +, −, x, ÷

35

Division: Zero And One

Directions: Study the rules of division and the examples. Divide, then write the number of the rule you used to solve each problem.

Examples:

Rule 1: 1)5 (5)   Any number divided by 1 is that number.

Rule 2: 5)5 (1)   Any number except 0 divided by itself is 1.

Rule 3: 7)0 (0)   Zero divided by any number is zero.

Rule 4: 0)7   You cannot divide by zero.

1)6 (6)   Rule _1_

4 ÷ 1 = _4_   Rule _1_

7)7 (1)   Rule _2_

ZERO ONE

9 ÷ 9 = _1_   Rule _2_

9)0 (0)   Rule _3_

7 ÷ 1 = _7_   Rule _1_

1)4 (4)   Rule _1_

6 ÷ 0 = ___   Rule _4_

38

Review

Directions: Multiply or divide. Fill in the blanks with the missing numbers or x or ÷ signs. The first one is done for you.

5 x 4 = 20

5 x 4 = 20

6 x 8 = _48_

7 x _2_ = 14

3 _x_ 6 = 18

7 x 2 = _14_

_8_ x 3 = 24

6 ÷ 2 = 3

24 ÷ 6 = _4_

6 x 5 = _30_

25 ÷ 5 = 5

49 ÷ 7 = _7_

8 x _4_ = 32

3 x 8 = 24

18 ÷ 3 = _6_

9 x 5 = _45_

12 ÷ 3 = 4

9 x 8 = _72_

6 x _6_ = 36

36

Division: Remainders

Division is a way to find out how many times one number is contained in another number. For example, 28 ÷ 4 = 7 means that there are seven groups of four in 28. The dividend is the larger number that is divided by the smaller number, or divisor. The quotient is the answer in a division problem. The remainder is the amount left over. The remainder is always less than the divisor.

Directions: Study the example. Find each quotient and remainder.

Example:

There are 11 dog biscuits.
Put them in groups of 3.
There are 2 left over.

3)11 (3)   3)11 (3 r 2)
  -9
  2 remainder

Remember: The remainder must be less than the **divisor**!

3)13 (4 r 1)   4)17 (4 r 1)   6)32 (5 r 2)   5)26 (5 r 1)

9 ÷ 4 = _2 r 1_   12 ÷ 5 = _2 r 2_   26 ÷ 4 = _6 r 2_   49 ÷ 9 = _5 r 4_

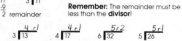

The pet store has 7 cats.
Two cats go in each
cage. How many cats
are left over?   _1_

39

114

Multiples

Name: _____

Directions: Draw a red circle around the numbers that can be divided by 2. We say these are multiples of 2.
Draw a blue **X** on the multiples of 3.
Draw a green square around the multiples of 5.
Draw a yellow circle around the multiples of 10.

circles: yellow and red

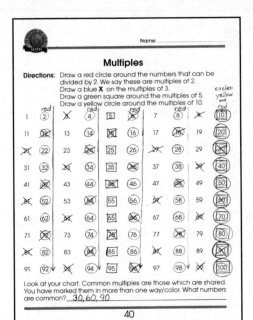

Look at your chart. Common multiples are those which are shared. You have marked them in more than one way/color. What numbers are common? _30, 60, 90_

40

Percentages

Name: _____

A percentage is the amount of a number out of 100. This is the percent sign: %

Directions: Fill in the blanks.

Example: 70% = $\frac{70}{100}$ $\frac{40}{}$ % = $\frac{40}{100}$

30% = $\frac{30}{100}$ 10% = $\frac{10}{100}$

90% = $\frac{90}{100}$ 40% = $\frac{40}{100}$

70% = $\frac{70}{100}$ 80% = $\frac{80}{100}$

_20_ % = $\frac{20}{100}$ _60_ % = $\frac{60}{100}$

_30_ % = $\frac{30}{100}$ _10_ % = $\frac{10}{100}$

_50_ % = $\frac{50}{100}$ _90_ % = $\frac{90}{100}$

43

Divisibility Rules

Name: _____

A number is divisible... by 2 if the last digit is 0 or even (2, 4, 6, 8).
by 3 if the sum of all digits is divisible by 3.
by 4 if the last two digits are divisible by 4.
by 5 if the last digit is a 0 or 5.
by 10 if the last digit is 0.

Example: 250 is divisible by _2, 5, 10_

Directions: Tell what numbers each of these numbers is divisible by.

3,732 _2, 3, 4_   439 _—_

50 _2, 5, 10_   444 _2, 3, 4_

7,960 _2, 4, 5, 10_   8,212 _2, 4_

104,924 _2, 4_   2,345 _5_

41

Fractions

Name: _____

A fraction is a number that names part of a whole, such as $\frac{1}{2}$ or $\frac{1}{3}$.

Directions: Write the fraction that tells what part of each figure is colored. The first one is done for you.

Example: $\frac{2}{5}$ parts shaded
5 parts in the whole figure

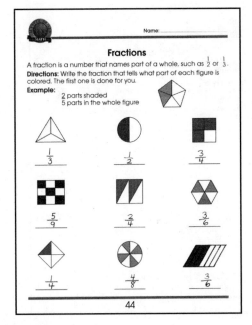

$\frac{1}{3}$ $\frac{1}{2}$ $\frac{3}{4}$

$\frac{5}{9}$ $\frac{2}{4}$ $\frac{3}{6}$

$\frac{1}{4}$ $\frac{4}{8}$ $\frac{3}{6}$

44

Factor Trees

Name: _____

Factors are the smaller numbers multiplied together to make a larger number. Factor trees are one way to find all the factors of a number.

Example:

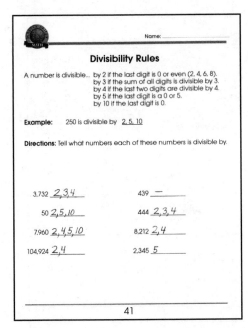

42

Fractions

Name: _____

Directions: We often use fractions in cooking or baking. Look for fractions you know as you use this recipe with your mom or dad.

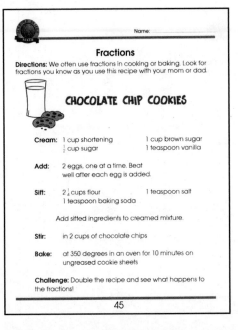

CHOCOLATE CHIP COOKIES

Cream: 1 cup shortening   1 cup brown sugar
$\frac{1}{2}$ cup sugar   1 teaspoon vanilla

Add: 2 eggs, one at a time. Beat well after each egg is added.

Sift: $2\frac{1}{4}$ cups flour   1 teaspoon salt
1 teaspoon baking soda

Add sifted ingredients to creamed mixture.

Stir: in 2 cups of chocolate chips

Bake: at 350 degrees in an oven for 10 minutes on ungreased cookie sheets

Challenge: Double the recipe and see what happens to the fractions!

45

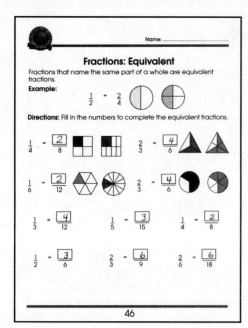

Fractions: Equivalent

Fractions that name the same part of a whole are equivalent fractions.

Example:

$$\frac{1}{2} = \frac{2}{4}$$

Directions: Fill in the numbers to complete the equivalent fractions.

$\frac{1}{4} = \frac{2}{8}$ $\frac{2}{3} = \frac{4}{6}$

$\frac{1}{6} = \frac{2}{12}$ $\frac{2}{3} = \frac{4}{6}$

$\frac{1}{3} = \frac{4}{12}$ $\frac{1}{5} = \frac{3}{15}$ $\frac{1}{4} = \frac{2}{8}$

$\frac{1}{2} = \frac{3}{6}$ $\frac{2}{3} = \frac{6}{9}$ $\frac{2}{6} = \frac{6}{18}$

46

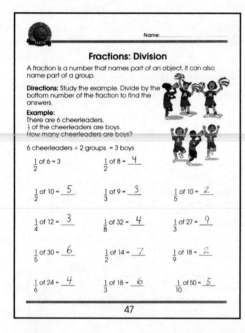

Fractions: Division

A fraction is a number that names part of an object. It can also name part of a group.

Directions: Study the example. Divide by the bottom number of the fraction to find the answers.

Example:
There are 6 cheerleaders.
$\frac{1}{2}$ of the cheerleaders are boys.
How many cheerleaders are boys?

6 cheerleaders ÷ 2 groups = 3 boys

$\frac{1}{2}$ of 6 = 3 $\frac{1}{2}$ of 8 = 4

$\frac{1}{2}$ of 10 = 5 $\frac{1}{3}$ of 9 = 3 $\frac{1}{5}$ of 10 = 2

$\frac{1}{4}$ of 12 = 3 $\frac{1}{8}$ of 32 = 4 $\frac{1}{3}$ of 27 = 9

$\frac{1}{5}$ of 30 = 6 $\frac{1}{2}$ of 14 = 7 $\frac{1}{9}$ of 18 = 2

$\frac{1}{6}$ of 24 = 4 $\frac{1}{3}$ of 18 = 6 $\frac{1}{10}$ of 50 = 5

47

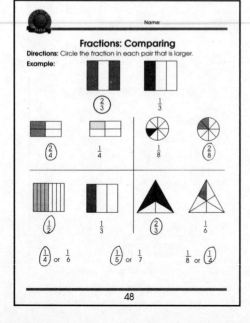

Fractions: Comparing

Directions: Circle the fraction in each pair that is larger.

Example:

$\textcircled{\frac{2}{3}}$ $\frac{1}{3}$

$\textcircled{\frac{2}{4}}$ $\frac{1}{4}$ $\frac{1}{8}$ $\textcircled{\frac{2}{8}}$

$\textcircled{\frac{1}{2}}$ $\frac{1}{3}$ $\textcircled{\frac{2}{3}}$ $\frac{1}{6}$

$\textcircled{\frac{1}{4}}$ or $\frac{1}{6}$ $\textcircled{\frac{1}{5}}$ or $\frac{1}{7}$ $\frac{1}{8}$ or $\textcircled{\frac{1}{4}}$

48

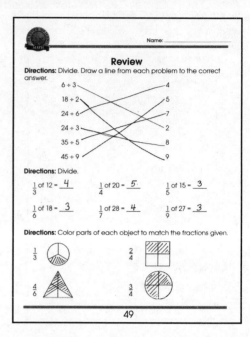

Review

Directions: Divide. Draw a line from each problem to the correct answer.

6 ÷ 3   4
18 ÷ 2   5
24 ÷ 6   7
24 ÷ 3   2
35 ÷ 5   8
45 ÷ 9   9

Directions: Divide.

$\frac{1}{3}$ of 12 = 4 $\frac{1}{4}$ of 20 = 5 $\frac{1}{5}$ of 15 = 3

$\frac{1}{6}$ of 18 = 3 $\frac{1}{7}$ of 28 = 4 $\frac{1}{9}$ of 27 = 3

Directions: Color parts of each object to match the fractions given.

$\frac{1}{3}$ $\frac{2}{4}$

$\frac{4}{6}$ $\frac{3}{4}$

49

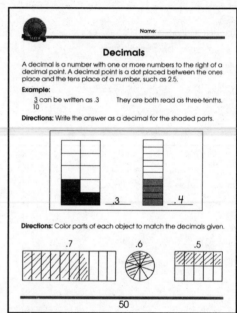

Decimals

A decimal is a number with one or more numbers to the right of a decimal point. A decimal point is a dot placed between the ones place and the tens place of a number, such as 2.5.

Example:

$\frac{3}{10}$ can be written as .3   They are both read as three-tenths.

Directions: Write the answer as a decimal for the shaded parts.

.3   .4

Directions: Color parts of each object to match the decimals given.

.7   .6   .5

50

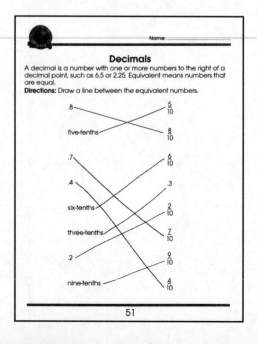

Decimals

A decimal is a number with one or more numbers to the right of a decimal point, such as 6.5 or 2.25. Equivalent means numbers that are equal.

Directions: Draw a line between the equivalent numbers.

.8 ———— $\frac{5}{10}$

five-tenths ———— $\frac{8}{10}$

.7 ———— $\frac{6}{10}$

.4 ———— $\frac{3}{10}$ 3

six-tenths ———— $\frac{2}{10}$

three-tenths ———— $\frac{7}{10}$

.2 ———— $\frac{9}{10}$

nine-tenths ———— $\frac{4}{10}$

51

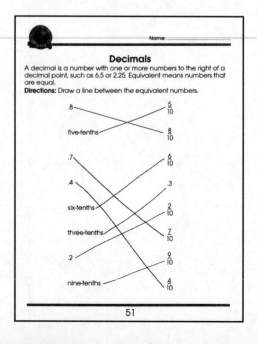

116

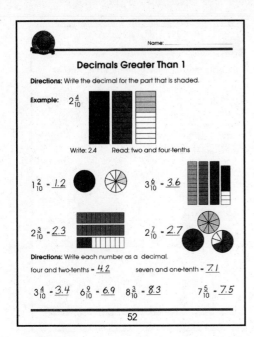

Decimals Greater Than 1

Directions: Write the decimal for the part that is shaded.

Example: $2\frac{4}{10}$

Write: 2.4   Read: two and four-tenths

$1\frac{2}{10} = \underline{1.2}$ $3\frac{6}{10} = \underline{3.6}$

$2\frac{3}{10} = \underline{2.3}$ $2\frac{7}{10} = \underline{2.7}$

Directions: Write each number as a decimal.

four and two-tenths = $\underline{4.2}$ seven and one-tenth = $\underline{7.1}$

$3\frac{4}{10} = \underline{3.4}$ $6\frac{9}{10} = \underline{6.9}$ $8\frac{3}{10} = \underline{8.3}$ $7\frac{5}{10} = \underline{7.5}$

52

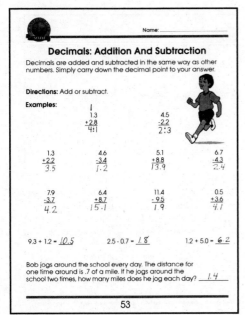

Decimals: Addition And Subtraction

Decimals are added and subtracted in the same way as other numbers. Simply carry down the decimal point to your answer.

Directions: Add or subtract.

Examples:

$\begin{array}{r} 1 \\ 1.3 \\ +2.8 \\ \hline 4.1 \end{array}$ $\begin{array}{r} 4.5 \\ -2.2 \\ \hline 2.3 \end{array}$

$\begin{array}{r} 1.3 \\ +2.2 \\ \hline 3.5 \end{array}$ $\begin{array}{r} 4.6 \\ -3.4 \\ \hline 1.2 \end{array}$ $\begin{array}{r} 5.1 \\ +8.8 \\ \hline 13.9 \end{array}$ $\begin{array}{r} 6.7 \\ -4.3 \\ \hline 2.4 \end{array}$

$\begin{array}{r} 7.9 \\ -3.7 \\ \hline 4.2 \end{array}$ $\begin{array}{r} 6.4 \\ +8.7 \\ \hline 15.1 \end{array}$ $\begin{array}{r} 11.4 \\ -9.5 \\ \hline 1.9 \end{array}$ $\begin{array}{r} 0.5 \\ +3.6 \\ \hline 4.1 \end{array}$

$9.3 + 1.2 = \underline{10.5}$ $2.5 - 0.7 = \underline{1.8}$ $1.2 + 5.0 = \underline{6.2}$

Bob jogs around the school every day. The distance for one time around is .7 of a mile. If he jogs around the school two times, how many miles does he jog each day? $\underline{1.4}$

53

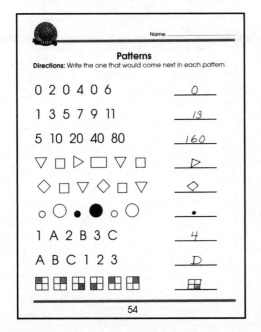

Patterns

Directions: Write the one that would come next in each pattern.

0 2 0 4 0 6 $\underline{0}$

1 3 5 7 9 11 $\underline{13}$

5 10 20 40 80 $\underline{160}$

▽ □ ▷ □ ▽ □ $\underline{▷}$

◇ □ ▽ ◇ □ ▽ $\underline{◇}$

○ ○ ● ● ○ ○ $\underline{•}$

1 A 2 B 3 C $\underline{4}$

A B C 1 2 3 $\underline{D}$

54

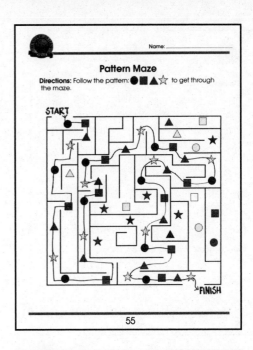

Pattern Maze

Directions: Follow the pattern: ● ■ ▲ ☆ to get through the maze.

START

FINISH

55

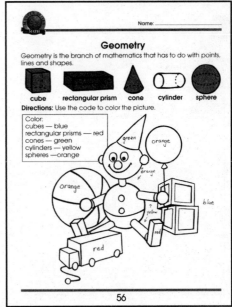

Geometry

Geometry is the branch of mathematics that has to do with points, lines and shapes.

cube   rectangular prism   cone   cylinder   sphere

Directions: Use the code to color the picture.

Color:
cubes — blue
rectangular prisms — red
cones — green
cylinders — yellow
spheres —orange

green   orange

orange

orange   yellow

red   blue

red

56

Geometry

Directions: Circle the patterns below that create a box when folded.

57

117

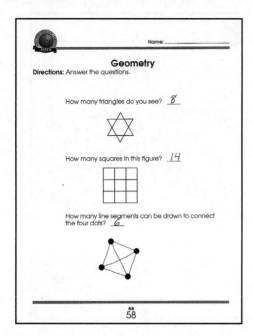

Geometry

Directions: Answer the questions.

How many triangles do you see? _8_

How many squares in this figure? _14_

How many line segments can be drawn to connect the four dots? _6_

58

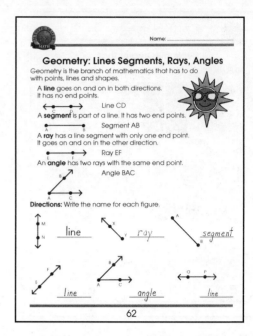

Geometry: Lines Segments, Rays, Angles

Geometry is the branch of mathematics that has to do with points, lines and shapes.

A **line** goes on and on in both directions. It has no end points.

Line CD

A **segment** is part of a line. It has two end points.

Segment AB

A **ray** has a line segment with only one end point. It goes on and on in the other direction.

Ray EF

An **angle** has two rays with the same end point.

Angle BAC

Directions: Write the name for each figure.

line   ray   segment

line   angle   line

62

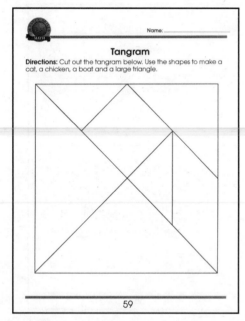

Tangram

Directions: Cut out the tangram below. Use the shapes to make a cat, a chicken, a boat and a large triangle.

59

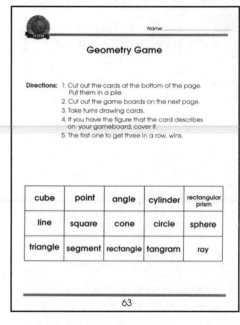

Geometry Game

Directions:
1. Cut out the cards at the bottom of the page. Put them in a pile.
2. Cut out the game boards on the next page.
3. Take turns drawing cards.
4. If you have the figure that the card describes on your gameboard, cover it.
5. The first one to get three in a row, wins.

cube	point	angle	cylinder	rectangular prism
line	square	cone	circle	sphere
triangle	segment	rectangle	tangram	ray

63

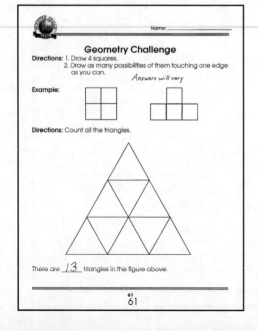

Geometry Challenge

Directions:
1. Draw 4 squares.
2. Draw as many possibilities of them touching one edge as you can.

Answers will very

Example:

Directions: Count all the triangles.

There are _13_ triangles in the figure above.

61

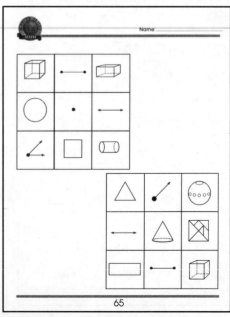

65

118

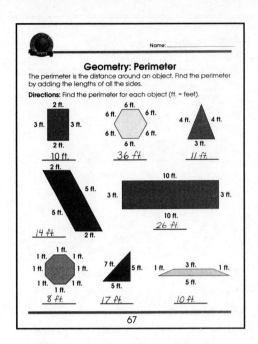

Geometry: Perimeter

The perimeter is the distance around an object. Find the perimeter by adding the lengths of all the sides.

Directions: Find the perimeter for each object (ft. = feet).

- 2 ft. / 3 ft. / 3 ft. / 2 ft. — __10 ft.__
- 6 ft. hexagon — __36 ft__
- 4 ft. / 4 ft. / 3 ft. — __11 ft.__
- 2 ft. / 5 ft. / 5 ft. / 2 ft. — __14 ft.__
- 10 ft. / 3 ft. / 3 ft. / 10 ft. — __26 ft.__
- 1 ft. octagon — __8 ft.__
- 7 ft. / 5 ft. / 5 ft. — __17 ft.__
- 3 ft. / 1 ft. / 1 ft. / 5 ft. — __10 ft.__

67

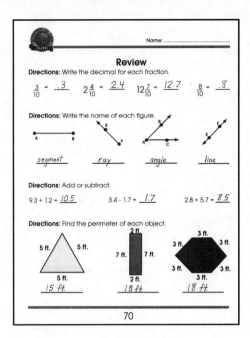

Review

Directions: Write the decimal for each fraction.

$\frac{3}{10}$ = __.3__ $2\frac{4}{10}$ = __2.4__ $12\frac{7}{10}$ = __12.7__ $\frac{8}{10}$ = __.8__

Directions: Write the name of each figure.

__segment__   __ray__   __angle__   __line__

Directions: Add or subtract.

9.3 + 1.2 = __10.5__   3.4 - 1.7 = __1.7__   2.8 + 5.7 = __8.5__

Directions: Find the perimeter of each object.

- 5 ft. / 5 ft. / 5 ft. — __15 ft.__
- 2 ft. / 7 ft. / 7 ft. / 2 ft. — __18 ft.__
- 3 ft. hexagon — __18 ft.__

70

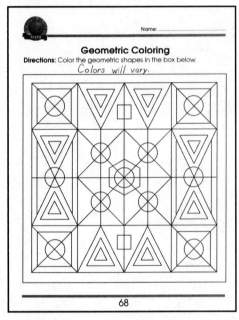

Geometric Coloring

Directions: Color the geometric shapes in the box below. _Colors will vary._

68

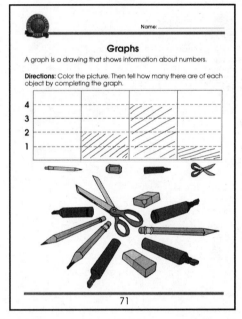

Graphs

A graph is a drawing that shows information about numbers.

Directions: Color the picture. Then tell how many there are of each object by completing the graph.

71

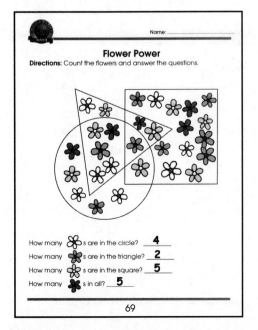

Flower Power

Directions: Count the flowers and answer the questions.

How many 🌸s are in the circle? __4__

How many 🌸s are in the triangle? __2__

How many 🌸s are in the square? __5__

How many 🌸s in all? __5__

69

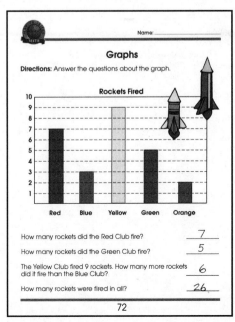

Graphs

Directions: Answer the questions about the graph.

Rockets Fired

How many rockets did the Red Club fire? __7__

How many rockets did the Green Club fire? __5__

The Yellow Club fired 9 rockets. How many more rockets did it fire than the Blue Club? __6__

How many rockets were fired in all? __26__

72

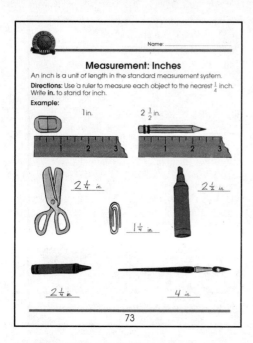

Measurement: Inches

An inch is a unit of length in the standard measurement system.

Directions: Use a ruler to measure each object to the nearest $\frac{1}{4}$ inch. Write **in.** to stand for inch.

Example:

1 in.

2 $\frac{1}{2}$ in.

2 $\frac{1}{4}$ in.

1 $\frac{1}{4}$ in.

2 $\frac{1}{2}$ in.

2 $\frac{1}{4}$ in.

4 in.

73

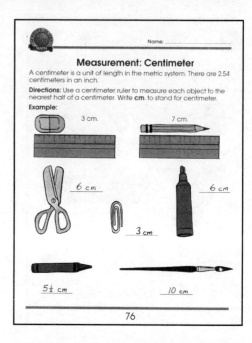

Measurement: Centimeter

A centimeter is a unit of length in the metric system. There are 2.54 centimeters in an inch.

Directions: Use a centimeter ruler to measure each object to the nearest half of a centimeter. Write **cm.** to stand for centimeter.

Example:

3 cm.

7 cm.

6 cm

6 cm

3 cm

5 $\frac{1}{2}$ cm

10 cm

76

Measurement: Foot, Yard, Mile

Directions: Decide whether you would use foot, yard or mile to measure each object.

1 foot = 12 inches
1 yard = 36 inches or 3 feet
1 mile = 1,760 yards

length of a river _miles_

height of a tree _yard or foot_

width of a room _foot_

length of a football field _yard_

height of a door _foot_

length of a dress _foot_

length of a race _yard or mile_

height of a basketball hoop _foot_

width of a window _foot_

distance a plane travels _mile_

Directions: Solve the problem.

Tara races Tom in the 100-yard dash. Tara finishes 10 yards in front of Tom. How many feet did Tara finish in front of Tom?   _30 ft_

74

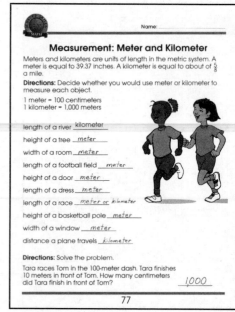

Measurement: Meter and Kilometer

Meters and kilometers are units of length in the metric system. A meter is equal to 39.37 inches. A kilometer is equal to about of $\frac{5}{8}$ a mile.

Directions: Decide whether you would use meter or kilometer to measure each object.

1 meter = 100 centimeters
1 kilometer = 1,000 meters

length of a river _kilometer_

height of a tree _meter_

width of a room _meter_

length of a football field _meter_

height of a door _meter_

length of a dress _meter_

length of a race _meter or kilometer_

height of a basketball pole _meter_

width of a window _meter_

distance a plane travels _kilometer_

Directions: Solve the problem.

Tara races Tom in the 100-meter dash. Tara finishes 10 meters in front of Tom. How many centimeters did Tara finish in front of Tom?   _1,000_

77

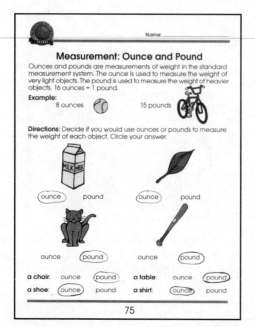

Measurement: Ounce and Pound

Ounces and pounds are measurements of weight in the standard measurement system. The ounce is used to measure the weight of very light objects. The pound is used to measure the weight of heavier objects. 16 ounces = 1 pound.

Example:

8 ounces

15 pounds

Directions: Decide if you would use ounces or pounds to measure the weight of each object. Circle your answer.

(ounce)   pound

(ounce)   pound

ounce   (pound)

ounce   (pound)

a chair: ounce   (pound)   **a table:**   ounce   (pound)

a shoe: (ounce)   pound   **a shirt:**   (ounce)   pound

75

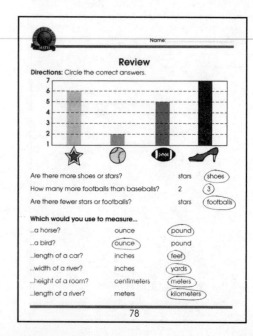

Review

Directions: Circle the correct answers.

Are there more shoes or stars?   stars   (shoes)

How many more footballs than baseballs?   2   (3)

Are there fewer stars or footballs?   stars   (footballs)

Which would you use to measure...

...a horse?   ounce   (pound)

...a bird?   (ounce)   pound

...length of a car?   inches   (feet)

...width of a river?   inches   (yards)

...height of a room?   centimeters   (meters)

...length of a river?   meters   (kilometers)

78

120

Coordinates

Directions: Locate the points on the grid and color in each box.

What animal did you form? _Answers will vary._

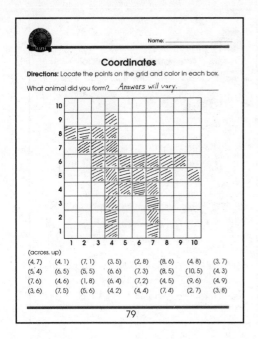

(across, up)

(4, 7)	(4, 1)	(7, 1)	(3, 5)	(2, 8)	(8, 6)	(4, 8)	(3, 7)
(5, 4)	(6, 5)	(5, 5)	(6, 6)	(7, 3)	(8, 5)	(10, 5)	(4, 3)
(7, 6)	(4, 6)	(1, 8)	(6, 4)	(7, 2)	(4, 5)	(9, 6)	(4, 9)
(3, 6)	(7, 5)	(5, 6)	(4, 2)	(4, 4)	(7, 4)	(2, 7)	(3, 8)

79

Roman Numerals

Another way to write numbers is to use Roman numerals.

I	1	VII	7
II	2	VIII	8
III	3	IX	9
IV	4	X	10
V	5	XI	11
VI	6	XII	12

Directions: Fill in the Roman numerals on the watch.

What time is it on the watch?
_3:00_ o'clock

80

Roman Numerals

I	1	VII	7
II	2	VIII	8
III	3	IX	9
IV	4	X	10
V	5	XI	11
VI	6	XII	12

Directions: Write the number.

V	_5_	VII	_7_
X	_10_	IX	_9_
II	_2_	XII	_12_

Directions: Write the Roman numeral.

4	_IV_	5	_V_
10	_X_	8	_VIII_
6	_VI_	3	_III_

81

Time: Hour, Half-Hour, Quarter-Hour, 5 Min. Intervals
Directions: Write the time shown on each clock.

Example:

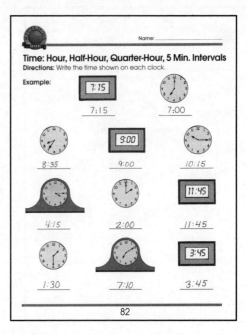

7:15   7:00

8:35   9:00   10:15

4:15   2:00   11:45

1:30   7:10   3:45

82

Time: a.m. and p.m.

In telling time, the hours between 12:00 midnight and 12:00 noon are a.m. hours. The hours between 12:00 noon and 12:00 midnight are p.m. hours.

Directions: Draw a line between the times that are the same.

Example:

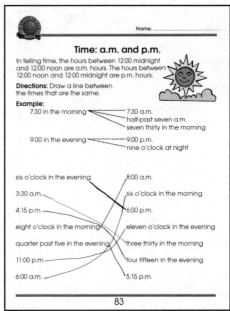

7:30 in the morning — 7:30 a.m.
— half-past seven a.m.
— seven thirty in the morning

9:00 in the evening — 9:00 p.m.
— nine o'clock at night

six o'clock in the evening   8:00 a.m.

3:30 a.m.   six o'clock in the morning

4:15 p.m.   6:00 p.m.

eight o'clock in the morning   eleven o'clock in the evening

quarter past five in the evening   three thirty in the morning

11:00 p.m.   four fifteen in the evening

6:00 a.m.   5:15 p.m.

83

Time: Minutes

A minute is a measurement of time. There are sixty seconds in a minute and sixty minutes in an hour.

Directions: Write the time shown on each clock.

Example:

Each mark is one minute.
The hand is at mark number 6.

Write: 5:06
Read: six minutes after five.

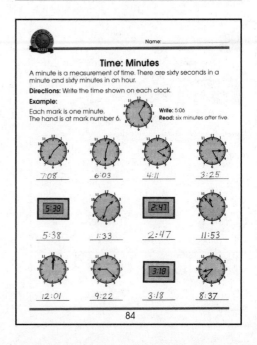

7:08   6:03   4:11   3:25

5:38   1:33   2:47   11:53

12:01   9:22   3:18   8:37

84

121

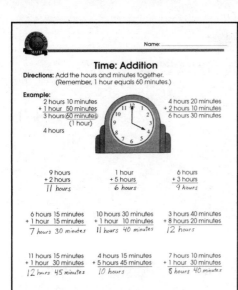

Time: Addition

Directions: Add the hours and minutes together.
(Remember, 1 hour equals 60 minutes.)

Example:

```
  2 hours 10 minutes
+ 1 hour  50 minutes
  3 hours(60 minutes)
        (1 hour)
  4 hours
```

```
  4 hours 20 minutes
+ 2 hours 10 minutes
  6 hours 30 minutes
```

```
  9 hours
+ 2 hours
  11 hours
```

```
  1 hour
+ 5 hours
  6 hours
```

```
  6 hours
+ 3 hours
  9 hours
```

```
  6 hours 15 minutes
+ 1 hour  15 minutes
  7 hours 30 minutes
```

```
  10 hours 30 minutes
+ 1 hour  10 minutes
  11 hours 40 minutes
```

```
  3 hours 40 minutes
+ 8 hours 20 minutes
  12 hours
```

```
  11 hours 15 minutes
+ 1 hour  30 minutes
  12 hours 45 minutes
```

```
  4 hours 15 minutes
+ 5 hours 45 minutes
  10 hours
```

```
  7 hours 10 minutes
+ 1 hour  30 minutes
  8 hours 40 minutes
```

85

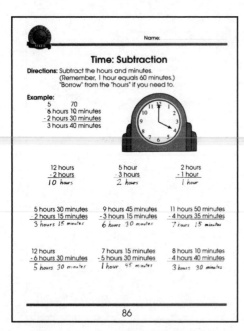

Time: Subtraction

Directions: Subtract the hours and minutes.
(Remember, 1 hour equals 60 minutes.)
"Borrow" from the "hours" if you need to.

Example:

```
   5   70
   6 hours 10 minutes
 - 2 hours 30 minutes
   3 hours 40 minutes
```

```
   12 hours
 -  2 hours
   10 hours
```

```
   5 hour
 - 3 hours
   2 hours
```

```
   2 hours
 - 1 hour
   1 hour
```

```
   5 hours 30 minutes
 - 2 hours 15 minutes
   3 hours 15 minutes
```

```
   9 hours 45 minutes
 - 3 hours 15 minutes
   6 hours 30 minutes
```

```
   11 hours 50 minutes
 -  4 hours 35 minutes
   7 hours 15 minutes
```

```
   12 hours
 - 6 hours 30 minutes
   5 hours 30 minutes
```

```
   7 hours 15 minutes
 - 5 hours 30 minutes
   1 hour 45 minutes
```

```
   8 hours 10 minutes
 - 4 hours 40 minutes
   3 hours 30 minutes
```

86

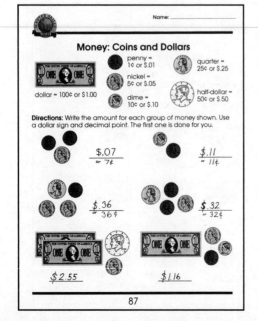

Money: Coins and Dollars

penny =
1¢ or $.01

nickel =
5¢ or $.05

dime =
10¢ or $.10

quarter =
25¢ or $.25

half-dollar =
50¢ or $.50

dollar = 100¢ or $1.00

Directions: Write the amount for each group of money shown. Use a dollar sign and decimal point. The first one is done for you.

$.07
or 7¢

$.11
or 11¢

$.36
or 36¢

$.32
or 32¢

$2.55

$1.16

87

Money: Five-Dollar Bill and Ten-Dollar Bill

Directions: Write the amount for each group of money shown. Use a dollar sign and decimal point. The first one is done for you.

Five-dollar bill =
5 one dollar bills

Ten-dollar bill =
2 five-dollar bills or
10 one-dollar bills

$15.00

$6.00

$6.35

$16.31

7 one-dollar bills, 2 quarters $7.50

2 five-dollar bills, 3 one-dollar bills, half-dollar $13.50

3 ten-dollar bills, 1 five-dollar bill, 3 quarters $35.75

88

Money: Counting Change

Directions: Subtract the money using decimals to show how much change a person would receive in each of the following.

Example:
Bill had 3 dollars.
He bought a baseball for $2.83.
How much change did he receive?

```
  $3.00
 -$2.83
  $ .17
```

Paid 2 dollars. $1.75

$.25
or 25¢

Paid 1 dollar. 83¢

17¢
or $.17

Paid 5 dollars. $4.35

$.65
or 65¢

Paid 10 dollars. $8.55

$1.45

Paid 4 dollars. $3.98

$.02
or 2¢

Paid 7 dollars. $6.38

$.62
or 62¢

89

Money: Comparing

Directions: Compare the amount of money in the left column with the price of the object in the right column. Is the amount of money in the left column enough to purchase the object in the right column? Circle yes or no.

Example: $1.75

Alice has 2 dollars. She wants to buy a CD for $1.75. Does she have enough money? (Yes) No

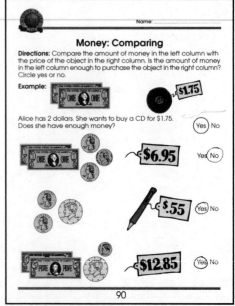

$6.95 Yes (No)

$.55 (Yes) No

$12.85 (Yes) No

90

Review

Directions: Complete each clock to show the time written below it.

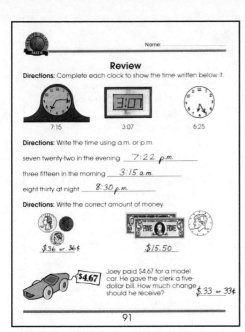

7:15   3:07   6:25

Directions: Write the time using a.m. or p.m.

seven twenty-two in the evening   _7:22 p.m._

three fifteen in the morning   _3:15 a.m._

eight thirty at night   _8:30 p.m._

Directions: Write the correct amount of money.

_$.36 or 36¢_   _$15.50_

Joey paid $4.67 for a model car. He gave the clerk a five-dollar bill. How much change should he receive?   _$.33 or 33¢_

91

Problem-Solving: Addition, Subtraction

Directions: Read and solve each problem. The first one is done for you.

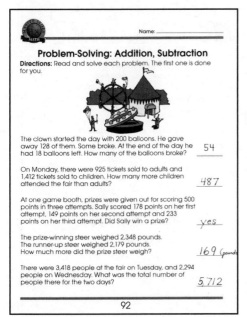

The clown started the day with 200 balloons. He gave away 128 of them. Some broke. At the end of the day he had 18 balloons left. How many of the balloons broke?   _54_

On Monday, there were 925 tickets sold to adults and 1,412 tickets sold to children. How many more children attended the fair than adults?   _487_

At one game booth, prizes were given out for scoring 500 points in three attempts. Sally scored 178 points on her first attempt, 149 points on her second attempt and 233 points on her third attempt. Did Sally win a prize?   _yes_

The prize-winning steer weighed 2,348 pounds. The runner-up steer weighed 2,179 pounds. How much more did the prize steer weigh?   _169 (pounds_

There were 3,418 people at the fair on Tuesday, and 2,294 people on Wednesday. What was the total number of people there for the two days?   _5,712_

92

Problem-Solving: Multiplication, Division

Directions: Read and solve each problem.

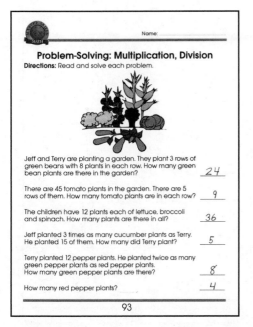

Jeff and Terry are planting a garden. They plant 3 rows of green beans with 8 plants in each row. How many green bean plants are there in the garden?   _24_

There are 45 tomato plants in the garden. There are 5 rows of them. How many tomato plants are in each row?   _9_

The children have 12 plants each of lettuce, broccoli and spinach. How many plants are there in all?   _36_

Jeff planted 3 times as many cucumber plants as Terry. He planted 15 of them. How many did Terry plant?   _5_

Terry planted 12 pepper plants. He planted twice as many green pepper plants as red pepper plants. How many green pepper plants are there?   _8_

How many red pepper plants?   _4_

93

Problem-Solving: Fractions, Decimals

A fraction is a number that names part of a whole, such as $\frac{1}{2}$ or $\frac{1}{3}$.

Directions: Read and solve each problem.

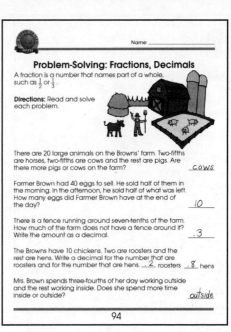

There are 20 large animals on the Browns' farm. Two-fifths are horses, two-fifths are cows and the rest are pigs. Are there more pigs or cows on the farm?   _cows_

Farmer Brown had 40 eggs to sell. He sold half of them in the morning. In the afternoon, he sold half of what was left. How many eggs did Farmer Brown have at the end of the day?   _10_

There is a fence running around seven-tenths of the farm. How much of the farm does not have a fence around it? Write the amount as a decimal.   _.3_

The Browns have 10 chickens. Two are roosters and the rest are hens. Write a decimal for the number that are roosters and for the number that are hens.   _.2_ roosters   _.8_ hens

Mrs. Brown spends three-fourths of her day working outside and the rest working inside. Does she spend more time inside or outside?   _outside_

94

Problem-Solving: Measurement

Directions: Read and solve each problem.

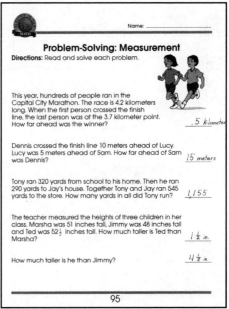

This year, hundreds of people ran in the Capital City Marathon. The race is 4.2 kilometers long. When the first person crossed the finish line, the last person was at the 3.7 kilometer point. How far ahead was the winner?   _.5 kilometer_

Dennis crossed the finish line 10 meters ahead of Lucy. Lucy was 5 meters ahead of Sam. How far ahead of Sam was Dennis?   _15 meters_

Tony ran 320 yards from school to his home. Then he ran 290 yards to Jay's house. Together Tony and Jay ran 545 yards to the store. How many yards in all did Tony run?   _1,155_

The teacher measured the heights of three children in her class. Marsha was 51 inches tall, Jimmy was 48 inches tall and Ted was 52½ inches tall. How much taller is Ted than Marsha?   _1½ in._

How much taller is he than Jimmy?   _4½ in._

95

Problem-Solving: Measurement

Directions: Read and solve each problem.

Ralph has $8.75. He buys a teddy bear and a puzzle. How much money does he have left?   _$2.17_

Kelly wants to buy a teddy bear and a ball. She has $7.25. How much more money does she need?   _$.19 or 19¢_

Kim paid a five-dollar bill, two one-dollar bills, two quarters, one dime and eight pennies for a book. How much did it cost?   _$7.68_

Michelle leaves for school at 7:45 a.m. It takes her 20 minutes to get there. On the clock, draw the time that she arrives at school.

Frank takes piano lessons every Saturday morning at 11:30. The lesson lasts for an hour and 15 minutes. On the clock, draw the time his piano lesson ends. Is it a.m. or p.m.? Circle the correct answer.

96

Review

Directions: Read and solve each of the problems.

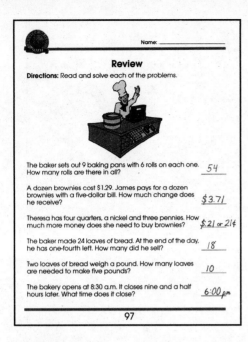

The baker sets out 9 baking pans with 6 rolls on each one. How many rolls are there in all? _54_

A dozen brownies cost $1.29. James pays for a dozen brownies with a five-dollar bill. How much change does he receive? _$3.71_

Theresa has four quarters, a nickel and three pennies. How much more money does she need to buy brownies? _$.21 or 21¢_

The baker made 24 loaves of bread. At the end of the day, he has one-fourth left. How many did he sell? _18_

Two loaves of bread weigh a pound. How many loaves are needed to make five pounds? _10_

The bakery opens at 8:30 a.m. It closes nine and a half hours later. What time does it close? _6:00 pm_

97

Challenge

Directions: See how many words you can make from the letters in the word "Mathematics."

MATHEMATICS

Answers will vary.

_____ _____

_____ _____

_____ _____

_____ _____

_____ _____

For a challenge, time yourself or race another person.

100

Math Terms Crossword

Directions: Use your glossary to help you fill in the words.

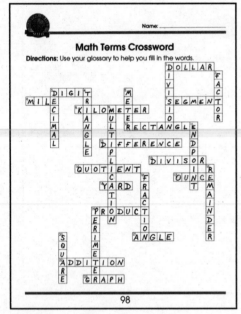

98

Review
Place Value

Directions: Write the number's value in each place: **678,421.**

_1_ ones   _6_ hundred thousands

_8_ thousands   _4_ hundreds

_2_ tens   _7_ ten thousands

Addition and Subtraction

Directions: Add or subtract. Remember to regroup, if you need to.

88	46	75	93	76
- 19	+ 39	+ 24	- 68	- 59
69	85	99	25	17

683	855	84	97	9,731
- 496	+ 138	49	54	- 4,664
		+ 62	+ 361	
187	993	195	512	5,067

Rounding

Directions: Round to the nearest 10, 100 or 1,000.

72 _70_   49 _50_   31 _30_   66 _70_

151 _200_   296 _300_   917 _900_   621 _600_

101

Math Terms Crossword
Clues

Across

1. 100¢
3. Symbols used to write numbers
6. A measurement of distance in the standard measurement system
7. Part of a line with 2 end points
8. A measurement of distance in the metric system
10. A figure with 4 corners and 4 sides
12. Answer in a subtraction problem
13. Smaller number that is divided into the dividend
14. Answer of a division problem
17. A measurement of weight in the standard measurement system
18. A measurement of distance in the standard measurement system
19. Answer in a multiplication problem
21. 2 rays with the same end point
22. Putting together 2 or more numbers to find the sum
23. A drawing that shows information about numbers

Down

1. Operation to find out how many times one number is contained in another
2. A number multiplied together in a problem
3. A number with one or more places to the right
4. A figure with 3 corners and 3 sides
5. A measurement of length in the metric system
9. A short way to find the sum of adding the same number many times
11. A point at the end of a line segment or ray
15. The number left over in the quotient
16. A number that names part of a whole
19. Distance around an object
20. A figure with 4 corners and 4 side of equal length

99

124

Multiplication and Division

3	3	9	9	7
x 6	x 8	x 8	x 5	x 2
18	24	72	45	14

5)25 _5_   2)6 _3_   3)18 _6_   8)24 _3_   7)49 _7_

Fractions

$\frac{1}{3}$ of 12 = _4_ $\frac{1}{7}$ of 28 = _4_ $\frac{1}{9}$ of 45 = _5_

Directions: Color parts to match the fractions given.

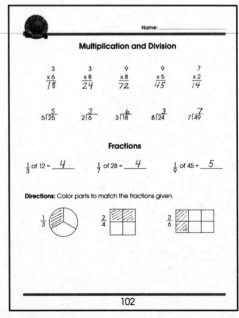

$\frac{1}{3}$ $\frac{2}{4}$ $\frac{2}{6}$

102

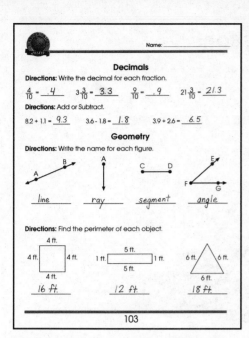

Decimals

Directions: Write the decimal for each fraction.

$\frac{4}{10}$ = _4_ $3\frac{3}{10}$ = _3.3_ $\frac{9}{10}$ = _.9_ $21\frac{3}{10}$ = _21.3_

Directions: Add or Subtract.

8.2 + 1.1 = _9.3_   3.6 - 1.8 = _1.8_   3.9 + 2.6 = _6.5_

Geometry

Directions: Write the name for each figure.

A ————— B _line_   A ↓ _ray_   C ——— D _segment_   F E G _angle_

Directions: Find the perimeter of each object.

4 ft. / 4 ft. / 4 ft. / 4 ft. — _16 ft._

5 ft. / 1 ft. / 1 ft. / 5 ft. — _12 ft._

6 ft. / 6 ft. / 6 ft. — _18 ft._

103

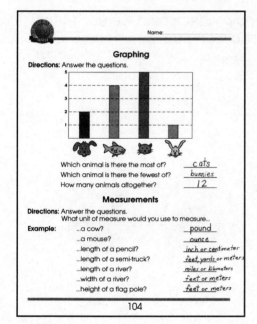

Graphing

Directions: Answer the questions.

Which animal is there the most of? _cats_
Which animal is there the fewest of? _bunnies_
How many animals altogether? _12_

Measurements

Directions: Answer the questions.
What unit of measure would you use to measure...

Example: ...a cow? _pound_
...a mouse? _ounce_
...length of a pencil? _inch or centimeter_
...length of a semi-truck? _feet, yards or meters_
...length of a river? _miles or kilometers_
...width of a river? _feet or meters_
...height of a flag pole? _feet or meters_

104

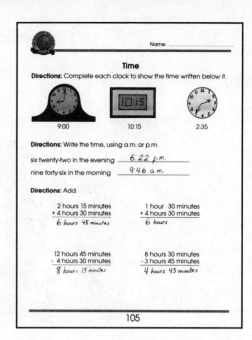

Time

Directions: Complete each clock to show the time written below it.

9:00   10:15   2:35

Directions: Write the time, using a.m. or p.m.

six twenty-two in the evening _6:22 p.m._
nine forty-six in the morning _9:46 a.m._

Directions: Add.

```
  2 hours 15 minutes        1 hour  30 minutes
+ 4 hours 30 minutes      + 4 hours 30 minutes
  6 hours  45 minutes        6 hours

 12 hours 45 minutes        8 hours 30 minutes
- 4 hours 30 minutes      - 3 hours 45 minutes
  8 hours 15 minutes        4 hours 45 minutes
```

105

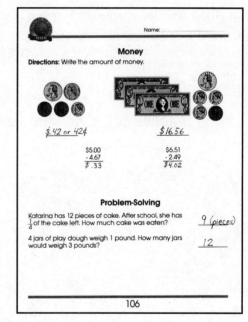

Money

Directions: Write the amount of money.

_$.42 or 42¢_   _$16.56_

```
  $5.00        $6.51
- 4.67       - 2.49
  $ .33        $4.02
```

Problem-Solving

Katarina has 12 pieces of cake. After school, she has $\frac{1}{4}$ of the cake left. How much cake was eaten?   _9 (pieces)_

4 jars of play dough weigh 1 pound. How many jars would weigh 3 pounds?   _12_

106

Teaching Suggestions

Money

Talk with your child about different things he/she can do to earn money.

Pose this question to your child: If we did not have money, what would we use to buy things? Tell your child about the Native American system of using wampum as "money." Do research together about other monetary systems.

Make money dominoes together.

Let your child practice coins with amounts of money.

Time

Talk with your child about different methods of keeping time, such as with clocks, stopwatches, calendars, etc. Let your child make a list of as many ways to keep time as he/she can.

Have your child time how long it takes the family to eat dinner. Have him/her write down the start time, the stop time and subtract.

Have your child make a "time management" chart to plan his/her time from after school until bedtime.

Teaching Suggestions

Addition, Subtraction, Multiplication, Division

Have your child compute his/her age in years, in months and in days. Then try your age!

Purchase a blank book or notebook to serve as your child's Math Journal. As you complete pages in *Master Skills Math* together, your child can write his/her reflections about what he/she has learned. If your child wants, you can write comments to him/her in the book to give your child positive feedback and reinforce the skill learned.

Talk with your child about how math is used in your profession. Make a list of other occupations, and talk about how math is used in these professions as well.

Imagine that "National Math Day" has become a holiday. Ask your child: If you were in charge of the celebration, what "Math Events" would you plan?

Measurement

Discuss with your child instruments other than rulers which are used to measure (thermometer, calendar, clock, etc.).

Let your child make predictions about the length and weight of various object around your house. Then have him/her measure the objects to find their actual length or weight. For an extension of this activity, try measuring the same objects with metric measuring tools.

Graphing

Graph the birthdays in your family by the months in which family members were born. Then ask your child questions to help him/her interpret the graph: In which month(s) do most family members have birthdays? In which month(s) are there the fewest number of birthdays? etc.

Graph the favorite foods of family members, or record the foods your family has eaten over the course of a week, and graph them by food groups. Have your child suggest other things to graph.

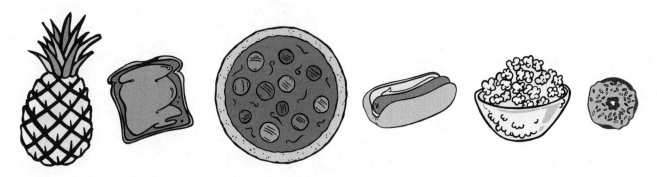